D0186857

*Ride on the Wind*

THE AUTHOR AND HIS PLANE AT SYDNEY

# *Ride on the Wind*

BY

FRANCIS CHICHESTER

With an Introduction by
Giles Chichester

PARAGON HOUSE / NEW YORK

First Paragon House edition, 1989

Published in the United States by

Paragon House Publishers
90 Fifth Avenue
New York, NY 10011



Library of Congress Cataloging-in-Publication Data

Chichester, Francis, Sir, 1901–1972.
Ride on the wind / by Francis Chichester : with an introduction by Giles Chichester.—1st Paragon House ed.
p. cm.
Reprint. Originally published: London : H. Hamilton, c1936.
ISBN 1-55778-223-7
1. Aeronautics—Flights. 2. Chichester, Francis, Sir, 1901–1972.
I. Title.
TL721.C5C44 1989
629.13′09—dc19 88-26777
CIP

Manufactured in the Untied States of America

# CONTENTS

## *ILLUSTRATIONS AND MAPS*

# INTRODUCTION

There is a romantic theme running through all of my father's adventures. It is the eternal quest to see what lies on the other side of the hill, over the horizon or 'round the corner, combined with the urge to be the first person to see it, the first person to be there and live to tell the tale. When my father took up flying in 1929, he had already led a pretty adventurous life for ten years in New Zealand. It must have seemed a fairly wild, frontier country to someone brought up in the sleepy, secure depths of North Devon in England.

My father took up flying as an extension of his business activities in New Zealand when the aviation company he had founded with his partner, Geoffrey Goodwin, lost money giving joy rides because their pilots kept damaging the planes. He decided he would learn how to fly on the notion that he should do better than pilots trained on heavy, stronger military aircraft. One has to remember that flying was still very much in its pioneering days, especially for long distance journeys in remote parts of the world.

My father's first attempts to learn to fly were not

very successful, perhaps due to business and other pressures distracting his full attention. Eventually he decided it was time he went back to England after ten years absence to see his family, get his pilots license, buy an aeroplane and fly it back to New Zealand. This is rather an ambitious programme for most people, but to him it seemed the logical sequence of events as well as an exciting challenge.

Back in England my father visited his parents and sisters but it was not an entirely successful reunion as they rather disapproved of his brash, colonial ways. So he applied himself with great energy and dedication to his tasks on hand and gained his license and bought a de Havilland Gipsy Moth bi-plane. He also set about learning how to navigate, working out where you have to go to and then reaching your destination safely. The practice of navigation was to be a dominant theme in my father's life both in the air as a young man and, later, on the sea. Neither flying nor navigation were easy matters sixty years ago.

The Gipsy Moth was single-engined with two cockpits. It weighed 880 pounds unloaded and cruised at 75–80 miles per hour. The cockpits were, of course, open to the elements so it was like riding a motor bicycle or a convertible car for sometimes eight or nine hours at a stretch without respite. I find it difficult to decide whether the exposure was worse from cold, from torrential rain, or the blazing hot sun, having only been airborne in a Gipsy Moth for only a very few minutes myself. Each condition added to the difficulties to be overcome by the pilot.

The controls were fairly simple, as was the instrumentation. However two features of the plane brought home to me just how impressive a feat it was to fly long distances singlehandedly. The first was the rudder bar, controlled by the feet, because there was a permanent bias requiring constant pressure from one leg to counteract. It would prove very tiring for any length of time. The other was the necessity of pumping fuel from the reserve tank to the main tank by hand. This was most taxing because the pump was high above one's head on the upper wing. It was necessary to sit up, hold the joy stick in one hand and reach for the pump with the other while maintaining that pressure on the rudder bar.

My father made a practice flight around Europe to test the equipment and his navigation before setting off to fly half way around the world from Croydon Aerodrome on Boxing Day 1929. He had a few adventures on his way to Sydney, Australia which are recounted in detail in his first flying book *Solo to Sydney* so I won't repeat them here, except for one story which seems more significant in hindsight. My father had a little difficulty in Libya because he had to land at Tripoli after dark and was deceived by a combination of moonlight and smooth sea conditions. He ended up landing on a beach which turned out to be under water, causing the aeroplane to tip over and break its propeller. He was forced to wait for a replacement and during his stay he recorded, for the first time, his nightmare about a vision blackout followed by his crashing of the plane. You will appreciate the significance of this occurring in January 1930 on reading this book.

One could say that it was not surprising for the stress

and fatigue of these long distance solo flights to induce nightmares. It is, after all, nature's way of making the subconscious come to terms with what has happened or what might happen and a crash while airborne is a logical accident to be concerned about, although taking off and landing are the most risky parts of flying. I have experienced a similar presentiment of mischance on a sailing trip I was about to undertake, and it was borne out by our being dismasted some 700 miles out in the Atlantic. However my forebodings had featured worse, more permanent accidents which did not happen whereas my father dreamt in vivid and accurate detail about what was to happen many months latter. So I am impressed by the instincts of prescience displayed by my father and fascinated that he should not only have dreamt so many times about his eventual crash but recorded the fact so far in advance.

On his arrival in Sydney at the end of January 1930 my father found himself something of a hero as only the second person to fly single-handedly from England to Australia. The next part of his journey proved impracticable because his Gipsy Moth could not carry enough fuel to cross the Tasman Sea. Both my father and his plane then went by steamer to New Zealand where he immediately set about plotting his next adventure. It intrigues me on looking back and re-reading his early books about his flying exploits in 1929 to note that my father was seemingly unaware of the financial and economic crisis which was enveloping the world at the same time as he was trying to fly round it. It is also noteworthy to recall in our age of mass sponsorship of all forms of sporting activity that he was able to pay for his plane and expenses out of his own resources accumulated through ten years hard work in New Zealand. Once he had become better known my father was able to attract some sponsorship and literary earnings. But the business outlook for his enterprises in New Zealand during this time became bleaker and the shortage of money is a recurring problem in *Ride on the Wind*.

His next flight was to be across the Tasman Sea back from New Zealand to Australia. It offered him several irresistible challenges since no one had flown solo across the Tasman Sea from West to East. His plane had to be converted with floats to enable him to land at two staging post islands, Norfolk Island and Lord Howe Island, for refueling. To find these tiny islands in the middle of a sea two thirds the width of the Atlantic Ocean required skillful navigation indeed. If my father could not find them there was no fuel for a return and he would have to take his chances ditching in the open sea. Again as the detailed story of this flight was published under the title *Sea Plane Solo* in the United States and *Alone over the Tasman Sea* in England, I won't try to repeat it here. But there are two aspects of the journey which are significant and of interest.

First and most important was the navigation. It must be difficult today to fully comprehend just how different things were sixty years ago. Without the benefit of radio direction finding beacons, satellite position finding systems, long distance radar, and sophisticated radio telephones operated by friendly air traffic controllers you were very much on your own. The answer was astro-navigation by sextant observation but that was easier said than done. You need not only a level horizon but also to know your own height above sea level. This figure has to be constant while making observations and you also need both hands to operate a sextant. This is most difficult when flying single-handedly, but my father developed the technique of putting the plane into a shallow dive while making his observations. He timed them, noted his altitude, and made allowance for changing altitude. Add to this the uncertainty of not knowing whether you would see the sun through the clouds when you needed it to make an observation, changing magnetic variation along your path, and the difficulty of calculating the correct amount to allow for wind drift when setting course, and you begin to have some idea of the problems in finding a lonely island in the middle of a big sea. To get over the fundamental problem of flying what you think is the right distance, not seeing the island and not even knowing whether it is on your left hand or on your right, my father devised the method of deliberately setting off his course to one side of the destination so that he was sure which way to turn. It was exciting stuff, it worked, and he reached his destination after a few adventures.

One of these was the other aspect which interests me on looking back. On the third leg of the flight, from Lord Howe Island to Sydney, he recorded seeing vivid flashes like the dazzle of a heliograph and the dull grey white shape of an air ship which appeared and disappeared before his eyes. The logical explanation for this phenomenon was probably a combination of cloud formation and sunlight glinting off waves combined with fatigue from being exposed to the elements while flying for many hours. And yet to a later generation such a report would sound like the sighting of a flying saucer or unidentified flying object. This experience was described in some detail in the book which was written sometime before UFOs made headlines and one can't help wondering whether it was just imagination or that he was ahead of his time in observing and writing about such phenomena. It must be said that out at sea one's imagination can play tricks with what the eyes can see and the funny shapes and colours clouds assume in certain light. I have spent hours watching a dark cloud on the horizon in the belief it was land.

One thing that was only too real on his arrival in Australia was the injury sustained to his finger. As luck would have it my father met up with the only aircraft carrier in the southern hemisphere (or so they said) when he made landfall 80 miles south of Sydney. HMAS Albatros made him welcome and took his tiny aircraft on board but in the process he crushed the tip of the third finger on his right hand between the hook of the hoist and the wire of the sling because they took up the slack faster than he was expecting. This accident naturally caused him some pain and added to his difficulties. It might have accounted for the apparent ease with which he kept dropping tools and essential equipment into the sea when working on the engine or the float of the plane. My father also laboured under the handicap of being short-sighted. Today, in the age of the semi-permanent contact lens, or composite material for glasses of little weight and great strength, such a condition does not seem a handicap. But think back to the conditions in that open cockpit with wind and rain buffeting my father, giving rise to anxiety about his spectacles being blown off or water obscuring his vision. Not to mention the hazards of his working on the plane when an incautious move could easily have knocked his glasses off into the water. The point is that there is something else which the pilot has to constantly bear in mind and guard against. Because if one loses one's glasses enough times for all the spares to be used up then one is seriously crippled as I have found when sailing.

One re-reading *Ride on the Wind* I am reminded of the great difference between the language my father used sixty year ago when writing this book and the style he employed thirty-five years later when writing his autobiography. Many of the expressions, indeed the whole style of his writing is of another age and it illustrates how our language changes and develops in subtle ways without really being noticed. My father grew up in the Edwardian era when the British Empire was at its peak and Englishmen had expectations about how foreigners should behave towards them which were very different from today's world.

My father had his own idiosyncratic way of looking at life and this might account for the name he gave to his Gipsy Moth. Elijah was, of course, an old testament prophet and very definitely male. He finished his time on this earth by going up to heaven in a whirlwind and my father clearly thought of this biblical reference in the early days of owning his aeroplane. When visiting North Devon he needed several helping hands to keep the plane on the ground while taxing into position prior to taking off for the return flight to Brookland. My father described her as seeming to rise up vertically in the air because the wind was too strong. Because all seamen and airmen think of their craft as feminine, the plane became christened Madame Elijah. As you will see in the book she did not live up to her name at the crucial moment, fortunately for my father.

For the first two flights of what my father intended to be an around the world trip ending up back in England he had prepared meticulously. But for the third leg it seems to me he had become a little casual after overcoming the rigours of the first two, especially the challenge of re-building the plane on Lord Howe Island after it had capsized and sunk in the lagoon. I fancy that coast and island hopping seemed less daunting than the Tasman Sea. An instance of this was his expectation of picking maps as he went along which led to him flying one day without a map at all. That makes navigation very interesting. Perhaps what I am talking about was really the burgeoning of his confidence as the adventure unrolled so that he became less obsessive about details.

I would not want to give the impression that my father was totally casual. To the contrary, he always took the job in hand very seriously and would apply himself to it with total commitment. My mother observed of his sailing that he was never happier than when he was tinkering with a broken down engine or trying to solve some abstruse navigational problem. While making allowance for a female view of what makes men happy, it is true to say that my father would worry away at any problem until he could fix it.

The satisfaction and, if you like, happiness lies in achieving the solution because nobody really likes working on an oily engine on a seaplane wallowing in the sea. My father was just like the rest of us in enjoying clear, sunny skies and plain sailing conditions away from the confinement of everyday life for preference over rough going.

The sense of freedom my father gained on converting Madame Elijah into a seaplane was expressed forcefully in his book about the Tasman flight and it comes through time after time here. That feeling must have enhanced the adventure of flying over mysterious islands populated by cannibals and landing in remote bays. There seems to be a double reality involved which heightens the freedom and adventure with the contrast between the solitude of the flying and the interludes on land for overnight stops. Then a different reality full of people and problems intruded on the peace of air. I hope the reader will absorb some of this feeling and enjoy the yarn as much as my father enjoyed living it.

GILES CHICHESTER
1988

# RIDE ON THE WIND

## CHAPTER I

### THE LONELIEST MAN

I HAD crashed in Japan. Dozens of hands clutching at me, mauling. Why not leave me alone?

Lying on the sacrificial stone; a glimpse through dull red, people pressing round, a man bending over me, his back close. One horrible pang; such a pain could mean only one thing; they might have spared me that. A second dreadful pain; I knew, and felt the loneliest man alive; I was an outcast from among men; why had they not left me alone? I had no desire to live.

Stitching began. Sometimes I counted; but any life now would be only a terrible void; I was at the end of everything. I gave up resisting pain, pushed myself over and slid into unconsciousness. Next moment, in spite of myself, I was back again and once more counting, in, across, out. Swine! I was behaving badly, groaning, and so felt ashamed and angry. After the man finished, he gave me morphia. . . .

By nightfall I was still alive. Lonely fear returned and I dared not ask if I were whole; but presently a faint humour stirred; throughout the night, whenever I spoke, I listened for an incipient squeak in my voice.

In the morning I called Suzuki over; the only man who spoke any English, he had stayed by me all night.

'Suzuki, my eye – er – about my eye – '

'The doctor say he think you save that.'

'And – er – '

'He say he think you save everything.'

When I heard that I could not get well again quickly enough. I obtained a Japanese dictionary. '*Kirei musume*' meant 'beautiful girl.' '*Anata wa kodomo ga ikunin arimasu ka?*' asked of a nurse when they were all in the room was a great favourite.

'What happened?' I asked Suzuki at the first opportunity. I myself had no idea.

'You have wonderful good luck. We cannot understand. Nobody understands. Everybodies is quite close. One man is only ten feet from where you fall. They rush to pull you out before the fire catches. You must be dead. Great is their wonder to find you still live. Many sympathetic hands lift you; they carry you to schoolhouse. One man fetch doctor, one man send telegram British Consul. By time I back – we have rushed when aer'plen disappear behind the rock and then we hear it no more; we rush back – the doctor is already there. It was terrible a sight. I am nearly sick. Everybodies is so sorry for you. Everybodies prays to Gard for you. The doctor thinks you do not live for ten, twenty minutes. He say send you to Hama hospital. I think he is a little frightened, you know; he does not like that you die by him. He like better for you to die by other doctor. I think, too, it is better we send you to Shingu; this is very good hospital. Dr. Hama is very good doctor. I telephone to Hama hospital. All young men carry you to train, very careful. They carry you all way one hour train journey. Dr. Hama he looks at your wounds. He says he think you live. I ask him about these sewing. He says he thinks it all right; one place that amount too much of flesh sewn in,' Suzuki indicated with finger and thumb. 'I say, suppose you sew again; but he say, "No, better to leave as long as all right." He say, "Very bad job for other doctor, no nurse." I think so too. I see once then cannot look.'

'But the crash? How did it happen? What caused it?'

'They see you come along and immediately they remember this wires that cross these harbour from hill to hill. Now they have remove this wires that you do not cut, and they go round on ground. Everybody stays very still. Then they see you pass under. But no, at last second, the aer'plen rise like so. It fly straight into this wires. But it does not cut. No, it bounce back.'

Apparently the long span across the harbour had not only slowed up and stopped the seventy-mile an hour seaplane, but had bounced it backwards. Then the steel wires having cut through several float-struts or because the seaplane was hooked in some other way it was catapulted forward again. When the wires took up for the third time one float was torn off, the seaplane was tripped over, and it was flung to the ground.

'Then,' said Suzuki, 'the aer-plen, it fall into the road, and the float, it fall in water, splash!'

'I wonder why I was not thrown out; my belt was not done up. Go on, Suzuki.'

'For one second it sticks on nose, then slide down wall into the water-edge and it fall over sideways. Almost before it has finish, the men of my town are tearing at pieces to get out Mister Chee – chee – '

Curiously enough, this crash took the form of the nightmare I had had, always the same, perhaps fifty times; that my sight went black and that I was waiting for the inevitable crash.

Sometimes I thought the kindness of the Japanese would drive me mad; all day long they walked into my room; hundreds, probably thousands, came from far and near. They walked in, dressed in their robes of ceremony, black kimonos with, outside the kimono, an unusual black skirt suspended from the shoulders by two black bands; and I often came out of the doze I seemed to drift into against my will, to find them within the doorway bowing silently or perhaps with a faint hiss of indrawn breath; standing in black silk stockings with the big toe separate. They always carried fans; their straw hats they usually left outside.

Suzuki, when there, would introduce them to me:

'This is directors of the ice factory at Katsura; they pray to Gard for you and they send you ice every day.' And a two hundredweight block of ice would arrive each morning. On some days it had a message inside in Japanese; on others, a bunch of flowers frozen in, or some reeds and a fish. When there was a fish in the ice, I waited patiently for it to melt out, with fresh hopes every time that it would come to life; but it never did.

'This is lady who has hotel outside where you fall.'

'Tell her that next time I hope I shall arrive without messing up the pavement.'

This was a stock joke, always sure to bring down the house.

'Here is priest of Booda; they pray to Gard for you that you get well soon.'

'Here is headmaster of grammar school.'

Many of the people brought me presents of fruit, fans, dolls, photographs and enough *saké* to open a bar. I always tried to make them a little speech of thanks:

'Tell them I thank them for their great kindness and for their gift and say I am very glad they make a visit to me.'

But every now and then a wild unreasonable fury would swell within me; it seemed to be caused by an actual pressure on me from the weight of other personalities near, and it would rush through my nerves like hot fire until, scared of breaking out into violent speech, I would say, 'Please ask everyone to leave, I am tired and want sleep'. And I knew they were offended; yet how could I explain that I envied any animal allowed to crawl under the roots of a tree until healed of its wounds. The Japanese certainly could not understand nerves being on edge; and mine were, I sweated in agonies of apprehension if the nurse dressing my wounds twitched a single hair.

And over this dressing of wounds, of which I had about a dozen, I offended again; finding it at first embarrassing for the operation to be watched by women and young girls, I would ask them to clear the room. They could not understand such a barbarous rude request. Later I grew used to their watching, as I grew used to other Japanese customs and to Japanese food. One visitor I was always glad to see; the Shintoist disciple, a wizened up old woman, a charming old lady, whose prayers were like a long droning incantation; and all the time she glided her hands over my body, always in the same way, until first I felt soothed, then drowsy, and afterwards would drop into a heavy sleep, no matter how many were in the room, while the rice-charms she gave me to swallow never did me any harm; she also gave me Shinto tracts with an English translation headed 'Foreign Missions'.

I had a special nurse, a Christian Japanese, supplied by the Police; she was totally unlike any other Japanese girl I met; when not relaxing in audible slumbers, she spent her time reading my Japanese letters or showering me with knocks, glasses of water, medicine and ice; however, I must admit she was clever at catching mosquitoes. The other Japanese I met, with their precise manners, their jolly natures, love of a joke, and desire to please, seemed ideal. Their little figures were perfectly proportioned; they were soft-skinned and plump-fleshed, with doll's eyelashes, soft, dark slanting eyes and jet-black hair. They were the most charming, delightful, sweetest little women one could imagine, and made one feel it would be dreadful to have to hurt them. The Japanese men rode rough-shod over them, but in spite of this they appeared to be extraordinarily happy.

I myself never had my mind clear about the Japanese. On the one hand was their official treatment of me; '. . . It looked,' a friend wrote to me from Formosa 'altogether too much as if, having failed to bring you down in the Formosan mountains, the powers that be had staged another and more successful attempt at Katsura, which appears to be something of a death-trap! I was glad to have a contradiction of the report that you had been given no option save to land there.'

But of course, I had not been allowed to land anywhere else.

'We had been hoping that he would not encounter an accident when taking off at Katsura,' wrote Lieutenant Mitsuwa, of the Naval Air Force, to the Nichi Nichi, 'Katsura Bay is about 2,000 metres in diameter, flanked by rocks 100 metres high. The outlet of the bay is narrow and just in front of it is an island. It is an ideal port of refuge, but a very dangerous place for seaplanes to come and go.'

On the other hand there was the kindness of the Japanese country people after I had crashed; and the hundreds of letters I received, including one from Hayashi Sun, the interpreter of Kagoshima;

> 'Sir: Receiving the report of the mishap I have profound regret which never could be forgotten. I expected you will success as I said you "I hope you will success" when bid farewell on the beach. I hope you will buy fresh eggs with money that I present to you (I enclose a money order, ten *yen*, which you must ask for Post Office) and take them to make you healthy.
>
> Yours truly,
>
> M. Hayashi.'

Two days after the crash I turned to the idea of writing, and as soon as I could, I began: 'I've got to get enough out of this book to live on and buy that boat. Am going to inspect a fishing-boat here as soon as I can walk. Doesn't seem to be much chance of ever getting a 'plane to finish my flight. Rather a pity, because I feel my nerve is as it never was before, cold and hard it feels like, and able to take me through any flying difficulty.'

I had already written 200 pages in the cockpit while flying, notebook and control-stick in the same hand; words that, for me, rattled on their mark like rifle bullets. The smell of hot oil, the roar of the motor, the drowsy fatigue in the hot blast of air, the tang of salt spray down on the water, the exasperation of trying to make a foreigner understand my English or, when he had no English at all, my signs – these things were brought back to me by the words of my log and its changing style, its jauntiness after a good night's rest, terseness in a storm, incoherence as the flight draws on, monosyllables as fatigue sets in, and silence perhaps at the end.

But unfortunately most of it was only intelligible to me, and must be translated as faithfully as I could translate it out of the cockpit it was written in.

'. . . Stuff written immediately after the event is valueless except for data. Crude, disjointed. . . .' I wrote left-handed in Suzuki's house. 'Every flight is moulded into a perfect short story; for you begin, and are bound to lead up to a climax. Coming on to those islands out of the blue – what a unique sensation! As soon as you see them you feel infinitesimally small with danger tugging at you from behind fanwise or sucking at you – you're like a swimmer in a nightmare making frantically for the shore with the current sucking you away so that you can't reach it.'

I quickly grew better, but even then it was not all *saké* and luscious peaches: at times I felt bitterly humiliated at the thought that I had no right to be alive; that my life had been tossed back to me as carelessly as a bone to a dog.

'If anyone says man is master of his destiny, he lies, tell him,' I wrote. 'It makes me a little depressed at times.'

'... What a half-year since I left New Zealand! Well, I filled my contract with myself – to go as far round the world as *Elijah* would take me. Besides, I shouldn't get depressed; I should never have been content till I had found out what it is like to die.'

'... The Buddha gongs are good.'

## CHAPTER II

### PREPARATIONS

FROM the bridge of the seaplane carrier *Albatross* I watched the Australian navy steam into Sydney harbour; then with bated breath, like, apparently, the junior officers there, watched while the anchoring of the ship in position was carried out as if it were a major operation.

I sighed as the last anchor went home; it would be hard to find a more hospitable, easy-going lot than the navy; and to an outsider there was something mysterious, fascinating, about naval life; as though it were a secret society, with its intricate customs and traditions, and self-sufficiency. I envied them their sure life, so pleasantly laid-out.

I and my seaplane had been taken aboard six days before, at Jervis Bay, eighty miles south of Sydney, a gale having blown me off my course in flying the Tasman Sea. My hands had been damaged when hooking the seaplane on an *Albatross* crane. I had been in the ship's hospital for a day or two; then treated like two royal guests, by Captain Feakes like one, and by the wardroom officers like another; I would be just finishing a hearty lunch in the wardroom when the captain's steward would whisper in my ear, 'The

Captain's compliments, sir, and he is expecting you to lunch,' and the captain's invitation being of course a command, I would then have to go and eat a second hearty lunch.

Now I must go ashore and immediately set about preparations for the second half of my flight round the world; the first half seemed now to have been too tame, from London to Sydney; for the second half I was looking for the most interesting countries I could find, uninhabited, hostile or little known. Obviously if they had aerodromes they would not fill the bill; so I had had the luck to borrow a pair of discarded floats from the New Zealand Air Force and had converted my old Moth aeroplane into a seaplane; now I would nose round the world among out-of-the-way islands, and since, by the conversion from land- to sea-plane, I had reduced the range to 600 miles, I should be compelled to in any case.

I was very soon in difficulties over devising a continuous route. Every five hundred miles at most, I must find a river or inlet sheltered enough for a 1,150 lb. seaplane to ride out the night at a mooring, without being swamped by waves or blown on to its back by the wind, where someone lived who could understand my talk or signs, and where I could obtain some petrol.

Up the Great Barrier Reef was easy enough; after that I must decide for myself the best places to land at, by imagining aerial pictures of the coast-line as described in the Admiralty Sailing Directions.

In Dutch New Guinea I met my first difficulty. Merauke sounded all right; a steamer called there every four weeks; but where could I land after that?

There was Frederick Henry Island '... about 100 miles long and fifty wide ... everywhere low, covered with dense forest and so marshy as to be almost inaccessible'. The Digul River '... the most considerable river on the West coast of New Guinea. On the upper part, the natives were hostile, the boats and bivouacs being repeatedly shot at. Higher up, there are no difficulties in the navigation, if mosquitoes and crocodiles are excepted.'

'The Inggivake was also ascended for some distance. The natives were hostile and twice shot arrows at the boats.' Further along '... in 1913 there were eight feet of water in the channel leading to the Kronkel River. Birab village with a population of about 500 is situated near the mouth; the inhabitants were hostile.'

There was nothing nearer than Kaimana Bay to offer me the least hope. 'Kaimana village – can be seen from some distance on account of the Customs house with an iron roof, the flagstaff on the residence of the Assistant Governor and several houses with corrugated iron roofs.' That sounded well. But it was 600 miles from Merauke, and I must have some margin to allow for a breeze against me. I racked my brains; the only thing I could think of was to fly 150 miles along the coast, dump petrol in a creek, then fly back to Merauke and, starting afresh next day with a full load, pick up the dumped petrol en route. I grew quite excited at the thought of a battle with the natives when I came to fetch the petrol. I pictured myself lying curled up on the cockpit floor and cutting a loophole through the side for my double-barrelled .410

pistol. I'd have to let them get close before I fired. I must pour candle grease into the shot to make it solid. Hit at ten yards range with that, Mr. Blackman would find a nasty hole in himself: yet I supposed I could scarcely hope to bag more than one brace.

However, the Dutch Government through their consul, refused me permission to fly over New Guinea unless I guaranteed to repay any expenses incurred in searching for me. I was furious. Supposing I had to come down somewhere to mend a trifling motor-defect, I could see myself working for the rest of my life to pay for a week's jaunt of the whole Dutch fleet. I wanted no searching for me; hated the idea of it. No one was going to share the sport if I succeeded; I would get out of my troubles by myself or take the consequences if I failed. Later, the Dutch said they would allow me to fly through the East Indies provided I signed a form absolving them from all responsibility. They had cabled to New Zealand asking for a quarantee of expenses, and two of my friends, S. Grant-Dalton and Eric Riddiford, had signed a guarantee without my knowing anything of it.

Now I met a Dutch skipper who knew the Arafura Sea well, and told me that the port at Kaimana had been withdrawn. The next place after Merauke was Fakfak, he said, 700 miles along the coast. That, of course, was hopeless for me. He was a cheery fellow, short and thick in body and face, and looked as if he could tell a story in the club, put down a gallon of lager beer, or knock out a mutinous seaman, all with equal ease. He said that, if I were forced down in New Guinea at ten o'clock, I should be in the stew-pot

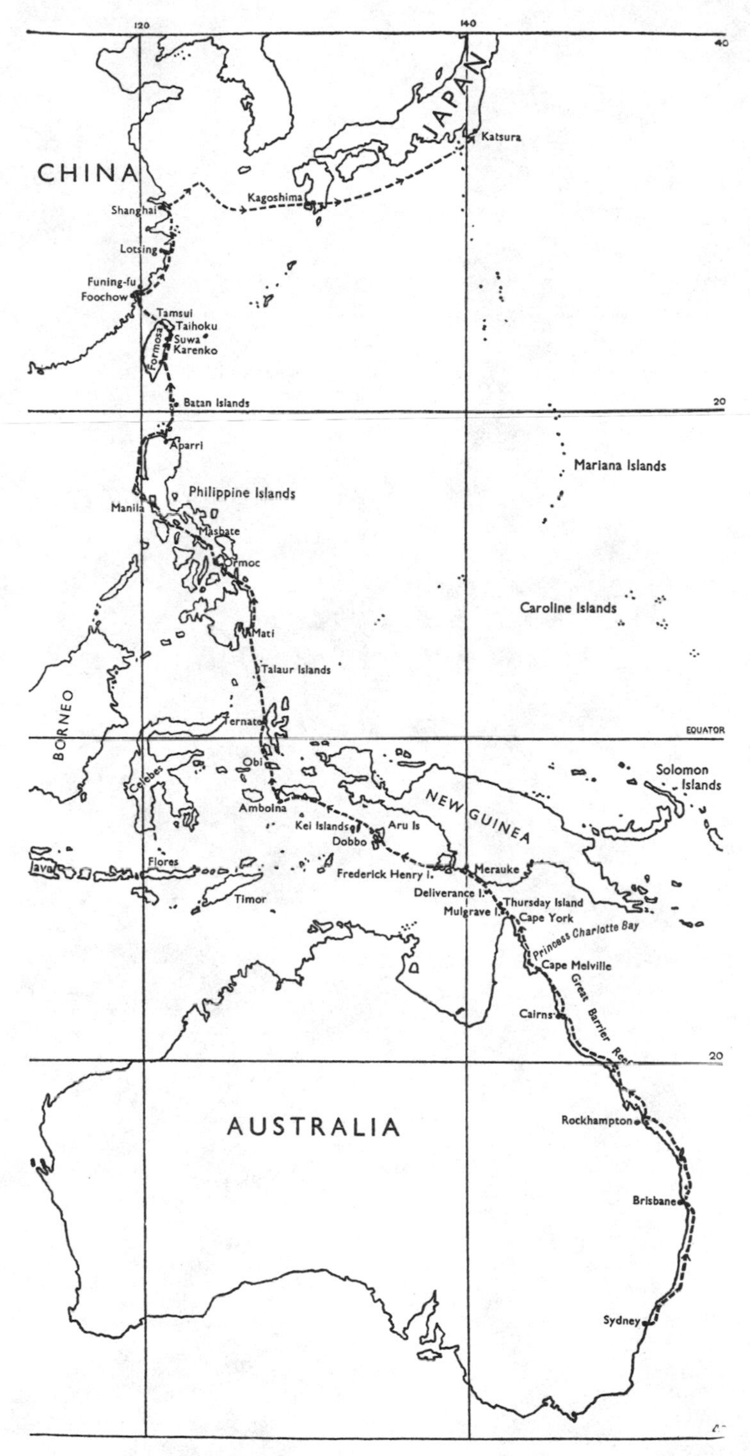


ROUTE OF THE FLIGHT

by twelve. He suggested that I should fly from Merauke to Dobbo, the pearling centre in the Aru Islands, a distance of about 480 miles, first over Frederick Henry Island and then for about 300 miles across the Arafura sea. Once I should have thought such a sea flight fearsome; but now I only felt grateful for its being within my range. Of course a seaplane, even as small as mine, was safer than a landplane if forced down at sea; it could stand as big a sea as a canoe, whereas a landplane was almost sure to sink, however calm it might be. Next, the Dutchman told me I should arrive at the Philippine Islands in the middle of the typhoon season. I had read in the Admiralty Sailing Directions the description of a typhoon; but thought that like most other things it would not be as bad in fact as in fancy. When I was told that few steamers could survive in the heart of one, I became thoughtful and went back to study the Sailing Directions again. I decided that the reason for my belittling the typhoon was that the word resembled monsoon. I now realised it was a nasty fellow. However, its centre only moved forward at the rate of some half a dozen miles an hour and, as I expected to be moving at the rate of 70 – 80, I fondly imagined I could easily dodge it, provided I received warning.

While I wrestled with consuls, De Havillands were giving my motor a complete overhaul after its night at the bottom of the sea and subsequent flight across the rest of the Tasman. Some of the pistons were cracked, the crankshaft was full of sludge, and the propeller-shaft thrust-race too tightly screwed home; but that was not bad considering the motor had been dismantled and reassembled at Lord Howe Island by amateurs. As for the first magneto, which had cut out completely for the last three and a half hours over the Tasman, nothing could be found wrong with it before I started. The other which had kept on spluttering and been so bad for my heart until I grew used to it, had a distributor cracked, and I watched the long blue spark jumping the terminals when it was tested.

Major de Havilland, or 'D–H' as everyone called him, was a man deliberate in thought and movement. He was very much amused at one of the islands I had chosen in the Kuriles, uninhabited except for three Japanese scientists studying marine fauna, where I had ordered petrol to be sent by the next boat passing; I must be sure to send him a postcard from it.

He probed steadily anything that puzzled him and then turned it over in his mind until satisfied that he had the truth. He frequently asked me why I was attempting this flight, which he considered impossible. I seemed to have a different reason every time he asked, which must have been most unsatisfactory to his truth-pegging disposition.

At the aerodrome he offered me a 'plane to fly. I hummed and hawed for a considerable time; the Tasman flight had shaken my nerve, and I stood for a while, watching other 'planes taking off and landing, moving away if I thought anyone was approaching to speak to me. I felt as if a fire had swept through me and left a burnt-up husk. At last I forced myself into the cockpit of a Gypsy Moth and took it up. I had developed a horror of being thrown out, and looked well to the safety-belt; but felt better after throwing the machine about in some loops and a spin or two. D–H and I agreed that the only way to keep alive flying was to be afraid. But there was a limit to everything. D–H was an interesting man, always having some theory or other to propound in his peculiar voice. He wanted to know why I did not buy a yacht and sail it round the world instead of flying. It was more comfortable, cheaper, safer and healthier. And at that moment, after a fortnight's contending with people and difficulties, it did seem to me like Paradise to be on the deck of a yacht, baked by the sun.

If only I could start, escape from this freezing climate that drove a chill to the marrow, from the infernal clamour and unnatural life of a big city, from the remorseless talk and the incessant scraping against personalities that grated on bare nerves like a knife-edge drawn across a plate. To fly north! To feel hot tropical air soothing and bathing one's skin with warmth; north again to the Arctic Circle, then to the right and east till I reached England.

Captain Feakes had allowed me to leave the seaplane in the *Albatross*. Now the flight-sergeant informed me that one bilge-compartment had been found full of water. It had not been discovered before because a chock had covered the drain-plug. This was worrying news, there must be a leak in the float; but the aircraftsman could not find one. I asked de Havillands to look when they remounted the motor; but their search was equally fruitless, and they screwed down the plate again after coating the inside with lanoline to prevent saltwater corrosion, which will eat almost visibly into unprotected duralumin. I was vaguely puzzled about the bilge, but there seemed no possible explanation and I allowed other matters to drive it out of mind. And hurry was vital – I must reach Northern Canada and Greenland before the ice closed the waters to me.

My finger, which had had the top scrunched off by the crane, refused to knit and irritated incessantly. I wished I could see the surgeon in *Albatross*; but that would take up several hours of precious time. At last I could bear the stitches in no longer, and walked up to the Sydney general hospital one night. It was pelting with rain and the cold perishing. The wind seemed to search my body with icy fingers. They were busy at the hospital, but an orderly volunteered to do my job. He was a fine figure of a man, over six feet, and broad in proportion – a grand heavyweight lost to the ring, I thought. He was very affable and willing, too; though the light was not good and his eyesight bad, he stuck gamely to his task until he had found every stitch and pulled it out with his pincers. I was standing up, feared I was going to faint, and cursed my feebleness in enduring pain. A seaman near by who had been knocked out with a bottle, put me to shame by keeping up a running fire of boozy jests while his crown was being stitched up.

At last I wrote in my diary, 'This place is no good to me. Nothing will "run" for me here. Every way I turn difficulties seem to jab stilettoes at me. The Japanese give no answer about the 1,100-mile water crossing. Perhaps I can wangle something when I reach the place. My finger refuses to heal and pesters me with irritation. Perhaps a little petrol and salt water will make it change its tune. The oil companies refuse to help me in any way. Very well, I'll find and buy my own petrol as I go along. If any place hasn't a motor-boat, it'll surely have a Ford car. I'll go and ask D–H for a loan; it's not pleasant, but money must arrive from New Zealand some time, and I will arrange for him to be repaid first, and any balance to be sent on to Thursday Island. I must leave. And what's more, I'm going to somehow or other. . . .' '. . . D–H turned up trumps. I leave to-morrow with £44 for petrol, oil, lodging, food and anything else I require on the way. What's the good of having a 'plane called *Elijah* if one does not put faith in ravens turning up when required? What a joke! It can rain cats, dogs and cobblestones of hell for all I care. For I'm away north in the morning . . . unrolling the coast like a map below . . . flying north, ever north . . . devouring miles like a bird swallowing grain . . . boring through distance . . . on and on . . . and on . . . sun . . . warmth . . . space . . . freedom . . . peace. I must obey this urge as surely as any swallow must fly to the south or die.'

# CHAPTER III

## 'ELIJAH' TAKES HER LEAVE

ON the eve of July 3rd I slept in Hewitt's cabin. In the chill air of early morning I stood on the deck and waited; Captain Feakes, though living ashore, was putting off in his launch to be on board when I started. While he watched from the bridge, the great hatches were rolled back and *Elijah* drawn up from the giant maw of *Albatross*. I tried out the motor on deck, said 'good-bye', and attempted to thank Captain Feakes and the others. He drew me aside and said, 'If you find it's impossible, give it up, won't you?'

He offered to have the 'plane launched for me, but I declined, mounted the cowling, and held the crane-hook under the sling-wires – treating it now with respect. *Elijah* was swung outboard and lowered to the harbour surface, smooth and sleepy under the weak winter sun, perfect and still. Odd wisps of smoke hung about buildings in lazy haze. Even the soft grey shapes of the moored warships suggested peace and safety in a placid existence.

But a glassy surface meant my seaplane would be unable to rise; it would not be able to unstick without a ripple or lop to roll air bubbles under the floats and break the grip of water suction. And with the

Captain on the bridge, with all the arrangements for launching completed, with my friends watching, it would be a horrible anticlimax not to get off. And, besides, all that fag of taking the 'plane aboard again....

I headed for the entrance. The water felt like treacle. I turned and headed for Sydney Harbour bridge. The seaplane would not leave the surface. Suddenly I spotted a ferry-steamer ahead. I swerved slightly and made for the waves of its wash. There was a minute island, with a kind of stone cabin on it, which I must not run into. *Elijah* caught the wash. I felt bump-bump-bump underneath. She was off. I was sorely tempted to slip under the bridge, which was prohibited, but it would have been rather ostentatious with my friends watching; perfectly easy, of course, since the biggest ships in the world went under, only that there might possibly be a rope dangling from the unfinished superstructure. As a result I barely cleared the approaches of the bridge; but did; turned, swooped to the *Canberra* first, dipped my wings to the *Albatross*, and then headed for the open sea. 8.20 a.m. local time.

I turned north up the coast.

Off!

Drifts of mist dawdled about the lowlands. The sea was calm and smooth under the eye of the sun. How grand! How marvellous! I looked eastwards at the thirty or forty miles of ocean stretching to nothing. It seemed to have finished with roughness now that I had crossed it. It was incredible that it could ever have handled me badly or was ever anything but calm.

'This feels like a holiday picnic. In fact the old

'plane is flying hands off the controls – for the first time since a seaplane. Queer feeling to follow a map again! and lazily enjoy the scenery. Roaring north! This is the supreme ecstasy of life. Nothing known to man can eclipse the intensity of romance and joy. I touch the peak of existence....'

'9.50. Huge school of porpoises.'

'12.20. 300 miles. The air is decidedly warmer; it gets right in and stirs the blood in my heart. How glorious! I haven't a care in the world.'

I shot over a ridge of dark green scrub on to a stagnant-looking lake. Thence down a way of water parallel with the coast. Skimming the surface a foot or two above it. Dark green feathery-leaved scrubby trees overhung the glassy water's edge. Wild, rough country. I put up two great flapping birds; would call them flamingoes, only that they were white; set after them in chase, at full throttle; caught them up, but heavens! they refused to dodge me and at the last instant I only just dodged them myself; put up another bird of the same species over dark secluded solitary water; followed it close. It could keep ahead at seventy, flying frantically with its great spread of jagged zigzag-edged white wings and its long legs of well-washed pink streaming behind, until, finding I gained at last, it checked in mid-air; when for an instant the legs dangled limply as if broken, before the bird suddenly crumpled, seemed to collapse, and dropped as if shot. Just as I expected it to break up and burst into a shower of feathers, it as suddenly took flying shape again and cleared off in a different direction.

I shot inland to another river – the Richmond, I think it was – and skimmed the surface for about twelve miles, parallel to the coast. Most of the time I was only a foot or two above the water and a yard or two from the east bank. The exhilaration of the flying stimulated and excited me till I felt half-intoxicated with it. It was an almost incredible delight that I had never been introduced to before, and it left the once considered marvel of landplane flying as a dull old show. Once or twice I had a sharp twinge of anxiety at the thought of wire cable stretched across the waterway.

This seemed to be an area of small farms, about the first sign of serious cultivation for four hundred miles of this desolate wild coast of dull green scrub and bush.

The surface of Brisbane River had an aged look; it was puckered and wrinkled by a breeze. A dull cloud pondered over the city in heavy consideration. I flew up-river to the bridge and alighted there.

Three o'clock. 6 hours 40 minutes. 494 miles.

## CHAPTER IV

### ROARING NORTH

BRISBANE was aeronautically cold; this gave me rather a jar after the energetic, friendly interest of Sydney people, where even the street flower-stall man used to call out 'Good morning Chich', as I walked down town. That was one extreme, of course; Brisbane went to the other. Even the hotel seemed bare, cold, and without any character.

'Yet, heavens! how people do talk endlessly, asking strings of questions. It is regarded as a favour, I think. . . . I enjoyed my dinner with Nichols, the petrol and oil agent, and did it full justice. Queer how one drink is about as much as one can stand after a flight; it seems to fire and run through every vein in one's body instantly.'

In the morning I said I must have provisions. We seemed to go up and down dingy, grey, deserted streets, for ever, in search of an open shop: at last we found one. The assistants had a sleepy, sour, Monday-morning look. The weariness and labour of their life seemed to obsess them. I felt as if I were buying groceries instead of provisions for an expedition, and came away feeling that my enterprise was only a futile drudgery.

The water police asked me if I had ever been to

Brisbane before. They said there used to be a man there once, the 'dead spit' of me, complete with beard and tramper's knapsack just like the one I carried my clothes and maps in. He used to walk up and down the streets begging, they said.

There was a bad spark-plug in the starboard set; also the compression in one cylinder leaking a little, due to a bad valve; an infernal nuisance.

'That take off! It makes my flesh creep to think of it. Yet it rather tickled my fancy, too, in the end.'

A foggy, light rain overlaid the river, itself a dirty-brown flow of muddy water with dull surface as smooth as smeared glass. Not a stir of wind in all the air. Impossible to have worse conditions for getting a sea-plane off. In addition, I could not see far ahead in the mist and small ferry-boats were continually dodging across the river, so that I had to steer a slightly swerving course from side to side for fear of striking one. Tricky work! I tried up-river, but there was scarcely any life in the 'plane by the time I reached the bend. Yet I had only forty gallons of petrol in the tanks. I tried down-river for the full length of the straight. I rocked her to mount the bow-wave, jumped and porpoised her, but could not shake her free of the surface. It played the devil with my nerves, watching the steamers and rowing-boats, buoys, moorings and ferries which loomed suddenly through the mist. I turned with slight difficulty, a man idly watching from the deck of a rusty-sided steamer that towered above me. I tried up-river again, went the full length of the straight, and yet she stuck. I reached the right-angled bend, and, though it had been drummed into me that a seaplane must on no account be allowed to deviate from a straight course in taking off, I had swerved slightly to obtain a few yards more run. My hand was on the throttle to shut off, when suddenly I thought the floats rode easier. It was maddening – just at the bend where I must stop. Then I had a hot, wild feeling inside me – and swerved hard to starboard. I could feel the port float lift; for an instant I straightened out the seaplane; swerved hard again; straightened once more; felt the other float draw less water. Still rounding the bend I lifted her off the surface – heavily stalled, but she was in the air and stealing upriver. Well! . . . I was learning something new about seaplane flying. What a joke – taking off round a corner! She took an age to pick up air-speed; I could not understand why; but at last had enough speed to turn in the river bed without mounting blind into the mist. I swung round and flew the length of the river to the sea, flying low with a sharp look-out for chimneys and masts.

Here I immediately ran into a heavy rainstorm which pelted me with stinging drops. 'Thank God I am in a sea-, not a land-plane,' – it was too thick for any course but skimming the waves, and that was quite bad enough even over flat sea, shut in by a smoke-grey invisibility always yielding to the seaplane's advance, yet always enshrouding and obstructing. Once I came suddenly upon a white wash of breakers along a narrow beach; another time to an abrupt cliff of red sandstone, and sheered off instantly with a rising turn to keep the dipping wing from striking the sea.

120 miles from Brisbane I flew into gorgeous

weather, immediately felt ravenous, and had a second breakfast. Sardines, wheatmeal biscuits, and a tin of pineapple, followed by chocolate. 'Must get a waste-paper basket for empty tins' – the slipstream blast snatched at the sardine tin as it peeped over the cockpit edge, and blew all the oil into my face.

I skimmed the passage between the mainland and Great Sandy Island for about forty miles. By Jove! Great Sport. I could see the bottom all the time with strong sunshine practically ignoring the water; saw one shark coming along – it looked a misty-brown colour. I liked jumping the flat islets covered with dark green scrub or tall bullrushes. I would fly up, skimming just above the surface till close, and then jump them, popping down abruptly again the other side. Over one islet I very nearly popped on to a rowing-boat with two men in it. I wondered what they thought; they would hear my motor approaching, be unable to see me behind the islet and then, suddenly, the 'plane would seem to stamp on them from out of nowhere with its great sea-boots. I could see the whites of their eyes staring at me and then I was far from them again. 'Planes were scarce in Great Sandy Strait, I expect. There were lots of swans on the water. I flew at them and within a few feet of where they drifted; they ignored me with a stately indifference, rather piqueing; they ought to think *Elijah* a giant marauding bird and scatter in terror. By Jove! this seaplane flying was the game for skill and thrill – if only there were not the work and loss of range. The marshy rivers looked just the place for crocodiles, but I could not spot any.

11.20. The brass screw-cap of the front cockpit

twenty-gallon tank flew off from where it projected through the fuselage. Fortunately the little safety-chain held it; but if that broke and it hurtled back in the slipstream I feared it could smash off the tail-plane – I wasted no time, saw a stretch of water underneath which I thought suitable, swooped down and round into wind; when just about to settle noticed a snag sticking out, swerved and dodged it. I was on a narrow strip of shallow water lying between a long island of sand and the mainland. The breeze was about 8 m.p.h. from the south. There was not a trace of man to be seen and I experienced an indescribable thrill; the uncanny silence and eerie solitude were balm. I was glad the cap had come off, screwed it on once more, and then let the plane drift till about to ground on a sandbank behind, when I started the motor and took off, after being down for about five minutes altogether. I made the forty-mile passage behind Cape Capricorn and so into the tropics; flew across a vast mud estuary, into the Fitz Roy River, and up that for twenty miles, reflecting that I would not change places with anyone in the world. I alighted in the river just below the bridge at Rockhampton.

360 miles. 4 hours 37 minutes. Total 854 miles.

'Left Rockhampton 8.30 a.m. Of all the God-forsaken holes. . . !'

It was hot when I alighted, hot, sunny and sultry. The first thing I noticed was the conduct of boats on the manœuvre; they barged and blundered into every launch or mooring they could find. The difficulty in coaxing them not to jab at my floats with their oars I was more or less accustomed to; but the petrol agent fiddled about till I thought I should never get to a mooring; and when I did, there was a can-buoy so close to the mooring picked for me that I had to stream a drogue[1] from one float to keep from fouling it. There were a number of craft moored out by the town front, but a more ungainly, crude, ugly and unseaworthy-looking lot I never did see. At last I got ashore, and was led through dingy streets to the best hotel – a back-country pub where I felt sure there would be steak and kidney pudding with apple pie for meals, a bed with tired cotton sheets and a clammy feel, tarnished fly-dirtied mirrors, and a poky back room with light from the bar filtering through the top half of a doorway where a ring of strong, silent men spent the day drowning each other's bad luck in pints of beer.

After lunch, I set to work – fixed the compass securely, changed four plugs, adjusted tappets, changed oil, and filled up with six four-gallon tins of petrol; finding it very awkward working with the bandaged finger of my right hand. It seemed to hit everything and get dipped alternately in oil, petrol, and Fitz Roy River, which is the colour of mud. No compression in No. 3 cylinder; always that infernal No. 3 exhaust valve. Could the camshaft or some such thing be out of true? I was very depressed at the thought of having to take the engine down again: finished at last and got ashore; but not without several arguments, chiefly with boatloads of youths who rowed up under the wings and held on to them for a mooring in the current. On shore I heard several uncomplimentary remarks about the Marquis de Pinedo, which I objected to. Appar-

[1] Sea anchor.

ently, de Pinedo, flying a twin-hulled Marchetti-Savoia flying-boat, moored there on his way north, and had trouble of some sort which delayed him. The Marquis de Pinedo was certainly a very fine pilot and, I assume, a gentleman. Perhaps his ways were strange to the Rockhamptonites. At any rate, if I now knew what they thought of him, I felt quite sure I also knew what de Pinedo thought of them! After tea, the oil merchant asked me to take a motor-car drive into the country to see something of it. My secret inclinations were towards bed, but I felt I must not rebuff a hospitable gesture: so was driven out a couple of miles or so to an isolated pub of which the proprietor was a friend of my host. Here I was sat on a beer-barrel, given a glass of beer, and asked innumerable questions. To bed at 9.30, tired out and bored to tears: decided that everyone spent so much time asserting their equality with everyone else, that they left themselves no time to acquire any other social graces. They have steam trams there, which puff like pot-bellied old men about the streets. I tried to photograph one, for here in real life was that very same Townsville Trolly of the Sunday comic page which makes the American children laugh. I found I had left my translation of the Odyssey in the *Albatross*; with nothing to read, I had no refuge from dreariness.

Next morning I thought I was never going to get off the river: racing up and down, swerving and rocking, porpoising[1] and jumping. There is something

[1] Porpoising - a slow rocking movement fore and aft which first puts the weight on the toe of the float and lifts the heel in the water, then lifts the toe while the pilot hopes the heel will not submerge as deeply as before.

indefinable about even one failure to take off which fills one with despair. At last I kicked her off the heels and trailed along nose pointing to heaven, heels probably scratching the surface, heavily stalled. I could not understand it. They had all said I should not get the same lift in the thin air of the tropics, but this air seemed to have plenty of body; it was quite unlike the rarefied belt over hot desert, for example. Heavy rain-clouds capping the range to the north drove me to fly back down the river again, before turning up the coast; I would not risk crossing blind: besides, I had difficulty enough in jumping the ten-foot river-bank, without trying mountain ranges of unknown height, not marked on my chart. I was soon in heavy rain, myself, and kept hard at work for sixty miles, when I flew into fine weather, felt ravenous and breakfasted again.

It was a marvellous sight, all the islands dotted about; I wished I could inspect one to see if it were habitable.

Now I was inside the Great Barrier Reef, though it lay some 150 miles to seawards.

Bearing of Molle Point from Shoal Bay 334° – for the first time I used my compass; but only to make the shortest crossing of a thirty-five-mile wide bay. I photographed a cane plantation which caught my eye with its lighter, brighter greenness as I opened up the bay.

12.0. Whitsunday Passage. 'That name stirs something in me. I wonder why? Surely it needs more than a name to set one vibrating with young excitement or whatever this feeling is. Anyway, I'm going to alight in Whitsunday Passage. I know I ought not to come down in such open sea; but I'm tired of doing what I ought to do in flying. I'm going to do something I want to do for a change.' The trouble was to find a sheltered spot suitable in every other way as well. A pretty fresh breeze was blowing up the passage from the east. Between Point Molle and the island alongside it was no good. Though sheltered I should be unable to get a run into wind for the take off. The Molle Islands further on had too much sea coming round behind them, I thought. Pioneer Bay, Grimston Bay, Double Bay, all had something wrong with them; either the land would be too high in front at the take off, or else the sea crept round, or there was insufficient run, or reefs showed their dirty-brown teeth. After having passed one of the bays, I decided it would have suited. This warm, sticky air made one slow-witted. However, I was not going to turn back to it.

12.15. 310 miles. I had now suddenly become ravenous as well and was growing irritably impatient. At last I came to Gloucester Island. The passage between it and the mainland suited me. I could lie in the lee of it and afterwards drift back for as long a run as I wished or work up water-speed in the passage so that the first big waves I struck would shoot the 'plane into the air at once. I made a swoop for inspection. Round again with a swirl, and down. The 'plane drifted back fast; in addition to the breeze, there was a strong flow of water through the passage. The line of drift was perilously close to a jutting point, where I could see a seething tide-rip; it had looked negligible from the air; probably a reef ran out there too, so I hurriedly cast anchor. For a while it dragged: 'jerk, slack rope, rope tautens, bump, anchor jumps free again. Perhaps I ought to start the motor afresh? No, the anchor holds at last. How stupid I am. The 'plane has only been drifting for a few seconds, or at most a few minutes from the time of alighting till the anchor held.' But, until the tension of body and alertness of nerves relaxed after flight, each minute had an hour's length. It was lovely there; the peace and calm and tranquil solitude. The Gloucester Island peak rose with scrubby green sides to my left and looked down on me with sleepy, careless indifference. A small boulder beach lay at its foot a cable's length from me. I sat on the front wing edge, dangling my feet and eating lazily. The sun shone strongly; the air was warm and salty and soothing. This was what I had dreamed of. Complete solitude (not a trace of human beings on mainland or island), ineffable peace, silence but for the slip-slap of wavelets against the floats – a strange emptiness of sound as if a nightmare had been cut short. The water had a colour new to me, as if a bright, clear blue had been mixed with milk, and I could not see far into it. After, I smoked a pipe and lazed on the floats or wings. A queer little fish with a wiggle to it amused me vastly. It was about two inches long and had a flat round end as if it had been cut in half and the tail end had survived. I watched it with interest, moving about the floats to follow it. As it continually wiggled up to the float bottom, touched it, turned away as if in disgust, and then tried somewhere else, I concluded it was a sucker-fish. The joke was that the little fellow obviously thought my float a shark or something else good for fastening to, and I could imagine his disgust every time he came up against white enamel. What a surprise for him if he did attach himself in hopes of a good feed, and then suddenly found himself flying instead!

. . . . . . . . . . .

Well, this would not do; with another 300 miles to go yet. I heaved up the anchor. 1.5 p.m. – only half an hour there; but what a half-hour!

I expected to make a dead easy take off; with exactly the right lop to the sea and a good breeze as well. To my surprise, the 'plane kept heavy in the water much longer than I had expected; and when she struck the open seas beyond the island and began bumping on them, she slewed suddenly to starboard. For a second I thought she was going over. I jammed on opposite rudder quick and hard. She righted and finally bumped into the air. 'Horrible! Cannot understand it. I must have been flying atrociously, yet did not think so.'

350, 400, 450 miles – the dreadful monotony of flying after four hours and until the nerves get a kind of second wind is indescribable. Of course flying like this, over shallow, tropical sea and with hot sun playing continually on head and shoulders was very different from flying at 5,000 feet; the sticky, salty air made one drowsy and enervated. It was the boredom and weariness of two days' life in the tropics concentrated into every hour of flight. And the lower the flying, the harder the work of pilotage. While yet another fatigue was the gorging of the brain with scenery, which continuously flashed underneath like a film four hundred miles long; until at last I was forced to turn blind eyes – I could stand no more for a while. And with the incessant roar, the blast of hot air, I felt I belonged to some other world, strange, hard, and unreal.

2.30. 450 miles. I had the greatest difficulty in keeping awake; I yawned so hard that it would not really have surprised me had I dislocated my jaw. When I could keep my eyes open they refused to align, with the consequence that I saw a double image. The sun nearly full in my face at the moment shot its glare into my eyes. I took several nips of brandy – about a teaspoonful at a time; rolling it round my mouth before swallowing: for I must collect my wits – I had actually left Rockhampton with less petrol than I needed to reach Cairns in still air, a distance of 623 miles; having such faith in the U.S. Navy's hydrographic charts that I relied on a favourable S.E. trade-wind – and was getting one; but, in spite of that, now realised I had cut it a little *too* fine.

Soon after I saw a beautiful little settlement on Palm Island. A large, low bungalow, with outlying huts dotted about a bay of cultivation, a patchwork of different greens, and the whole nestling at the foot of a sharp-rising hill and behind a beach of the cleanest-looking sand conceivable. Palms up the hillside; a lagoon in front of the beach and a reef. I was sorely tempted to alight there; I had two hours more flying and only two hours more petrol. I supposed it was a mission station, but it looked like the Garden of Eden to me. And what a surprise for them to have a seaplane alight at their front beach! I ought *not* to go on. . . . It is hard to say why I did.

'Seven hours out, seventy-five miles to go if I have to round Cape Grafton, sixty if I can cut across. The chart shows a mountain range there, but gives no height. There's not enough petrol for seventy-five; it doesn't look as if there's enough for sixty. I ought to try and alight near the first house I can see. . . . But the intolerable fag of worrying about the chance of a successful alighting in the open sea, and of getting ashore in my rubber boat; then after all that, the grind of refuelling at Cairns next morning just the same!' Besides which, the flesh-pots of Cairns, the avoidance of toil, called insidiously.

I began climbing so as to have a good long glide in case of need. The petrol-gauge showed empty with thirty miles yet to go, but I knew it did that while there was still some petrol in the tank.

I saw a break in the hills where I thought I could cut through; but felt too lazy to bother about the possibility of a forced alighting. I began to perspire hard at the thought of the bumping I should get among the hills – I should be bumped out – the wings would break off. I fastened my safety-belt and kept on looking to make sure the pin was in securely.

I was over the watershed. Not one single bump. Thank God! Thank God! . . . Cairns River lay within gliding range four miles ahead. I set the 'plane on a long slant for the river.

Eight hours. 623 miles. Total 1,477 miles.

Nothing along the whole coast resembled Cairns. It gave me a surprise in more than one way. From the air it looked beautiful, lying in a horseshoe basin split in half by the river, and almost encircled by ranges with a dark purple bloom on them. I expected to find it a sleepy, good-natured, gossipy little township.

The first happening as soon as I alighted was the rushing up of a launch loaded with passengers, who crowded to the side of the launch, clicking cameras; they had a rather silly, vacuous look, and I set them down as trippers. I felt like a man in a cage at the Zoo being watched by a lot of monkeys. When dead in my lee, they stopped the engine, and the seaplane promptly began drifting straight for the launch. I jumped for the wing root, switched on, sprang to the float and began frantically swinging the propeller, all the while boiling over with rage. The speech I made to that launch (fortunately indistinguishable) would have surprised a Thames bargee. I started the motor just in time and taxied well away. Busy rigging my anchor at a fresh spot, I happened to look up, and there was the launch right alongside again. Fortunately for them, looks cannot kill. The petrol agent arrived and told me I could not moor there; it had been ordered that I move right across to the other side of the estuary, almost out of sight from the town. I asked with wasted irony if they suspected *Elijah* of being loaded with gun-cotton. Next there was a long delay in obtaining petrol; I had to go with the agent to the storage tanks for it; so that after the tow across the estuary I had to finish emptying ten four-gallon tins of petrol by torchlight. On reaching the town again, the petrol agent told me he did not think I should be able to get a bed in the town. I thought he was joking – a full hotel in Australia at that stage of its financial depression! But to my amazement the first hotel did turn me away. So did the second; and the third. By now I was charged with gun-cotton – and on a hair-trigger. I angrily regretted ever having changed petrol companies. Gradually, however, I began to reflect that this was good for me. After the amazing hospitality of my hosts at Norfolk Island, Lord Howe Island, and in the *Albatross*, I was in danger of becoming spoiled. And at last, when Mrs. McManus of the Imperial Hotel squeezed me into a room which was almost part of the bath department and apparently without an outside window, I felt extraordinarily grateful: even more so when she fossicked in the kitchen and returned with some curry, cold meat, and Australian tea: a brew which is warranted to make one's hair curl. I gathered that it was almost a crime to expect any food at an Australian hotel after 6.30. Mrs. McManus, who sat and talked to me while I munched, told me that Cairns was full of tourists. After eating, I had a cold shower which was as soothing and refreshing as ointment on a sore skin. Then a bottle of stout and to bed at 9.15.

I had a bad night, sleeping fitfully, half dreaming, half thinking for most of the time, it seemed. I would just be dropping into sleep when a nerve would unexpectedly twitch like a plucked bowstring and make me jump six inches off the bed; or there would be a sudden intolerable itch at some spot. Eventually I lit the light and left it on, and donned the thickest pair of socks I possessed; they seemed to quieten the nerves. I was up at six o'clock, cursing my fate, and weighed down with self-reproach for undertaking this unutterably laboursome, wearisome task. Having touched the bottom of the abyss of depression, I proceeded to be thankful for and enjoy a breakfast of poached eggs. Mrs. McManus let me have a tin of sweetcorn, also bread and butter and jam, and a weekly magazine to read. Kindly soul! There was a New Zealander from Dunedin in the hotel, on his way to Cooktown that same morning by means of the *Morinda*, an eighty-foot twin-Diesel-engined motor-launch carrying mail there three times a week. I told him I would keep my eye open for the *Morinda* on my way north.

As only one bilge had shown water yesterday, I pumped but that one. No. 3 valve was blowing just as much, but no more; it had better not, either, for it would take a lot to make me dismantle that motor again so soon. I dropped the oil-level indicator-rod into the sea, and scattered curses in the air like sparks from an exploding rocket. It was a queer thing how, immediately the seaplane racket began, I felt rough, violent, elemental; that if anyone should stand in my way, let him look to his safety.

I got off the first time, the sea being nicely ruffled by a south-east breeze; undoubtedly I managed it by rocking the 'plane fore and aft till she had climbed on to the curl of her own bow-waves, and then, pulling back the control-stick hard and sharp, I forced her abruptly to unstick. I passed the *Morinda* which, with its spreading bow-waves, resembled an arrow-head shooting north along the now placid surface; I dived alongside, and photographed her as I flashed by; with a feeling all over me of being on tiptoe as I handled the controls with my left hand and sighted the camera with my right, the launch only a few yards away, the water a few feet below, the seaplane travelling at ninety.

'A gorgeous day: scarcely a ripple on the water.' All the air calm and peaceful and still, with only *Elijah* roaring north like the Bull of Bashan. 'Just getting my morning thrill.' It was as if I now bobbed up through the surface after having been ducked in drabness. 'Calm water, clear, dark blue, green. Brown coral. Turtle scampering. This amazing, glorious beauty would stab romance into a dying man.' Dazzling white strands of beach. The very salty green of barren scrub-land intrigued the imagination like the rugged features of an indomitable character.

9.30. Archer Point Lighthouse.

Here the Great Barrier had come into within twenty or thirty miles of the coast, and spawned innumerable reefs everywhere. The water over them was dark blue or green of utterly pure hue and the sun struck through to the reef below as if shining through flawless crystal. 'Some God must have flitted by here and wept copious tears of liquid amethyst; I can see them, still and vague-edged, lie on the reefs below. Turtle by the score take fright; they seem to float off the reef in every direction and settle away into the obscurity of the depths around. The reefs lie below, in various shades of brown carelessly blended. Lean, torpedo-bodied sharks, craftily like the reef in colour, loll lazily in the sunny shallows, as contemptuously disregardful of my roaring approach as any fierce insensible fighting bruiser.' One that I saw of mottled brown, I judged by my float shadow to be fifteen feet long. I saw a splash of water ahead like the impact of a dropped elephant and raced down to a blobby grey creature, the shape of a flat turnip, about twelve feet long, seven or eight broad at the shoulders and tapering to a pointed tail. It remained as still as a rock while I passed, and it would never have occurred to me that it could be a creature had I not actually seen it leap. I saw one big stingaree, flat like a diamond-shaped kite with one point slightly more drawn out than the other three. It, too, was of dirty, vague, brown-grey mottle. There was something horrible, ruthless and remorseless in the look of it. This sea was *alive*, with its purity of water colours, the sparkle, the dazzle of the surface: as live as the arid brown shore was dead. 'And this is where Cook, Flinders and Bligh had their adventures, their shipwrecks, discoveries; found safety and danger among these thousands of reefs. It is a romance merely to read the names on the chart; Three Isles, Turtle Reef, N. Direction Isle, Lizard Isle, Eagle Isle, Cook's Passage (1770); how I wish I had all the history of it at my command. And the amazing things to see. How I wish for three pairs of eyes and three brains so that I should not miss any of the marvel of it all!'

Cape Melville. 11.0.

For eighty miles I cut across Princess Charlotte Bay. For part of the way no mainland was in sight. I touched the Great Barrier and flew over scores of isolated reefs. Ravenous hunger seized me half-way. The front cockpit petrol-tank cap flew off again and, held by slipstream and safety-chain, pointed into the air like the raised upper jaw of a crocodile. I pulled out my walking-stick from behind my seat and, with great difficulty wielding it in the slipstream blast, pushed the brass cap flat. If it broke adrift, it broke adrift.

On reaching the mainland again at Cape Sidmouth I noticed a school of sharks in the lee of it, swirled about, alighted on top of where I had seen them, cast anchor.

It was hot; it made one's very eyes indolent. I took off many clothes and lolled about the craft; was much disappointed at not seeing any sharks; though sundry splashes which I heard (but always where I was not looking) showed they were near. I could only see the bottom just underneath me through water which obviously wished to be transparent, but was infused with brownish haze from the sandy mud bottom.

I lunched and smoked. 'A lean beach lies at the mainland; behind it, flat, bushy country. I see a wretched kind of shelter; the thatch has begun to collapse as if pouring through a hole in the roof. No sign of any human beings.'

I longed to fish, but had no bait; I even considered whether any of the tinned foods would do. I could not tear myself away. . . . Well, I must leave if I hoped to make Thursday Island before dark.

At 1.0 I saw a lugger ahead with sails drooping limply in the hot, still air. It seemed black from a distance – and I found it covered in blacks – as if the lugger had been birdlimed all over and they had stuck to it. Black! – they would have made a piece of jet look pale. It was an uncanny sight; for while the roaring seaplane flew straight at the lugger they kept as still as petrified coal; dotted about the deck, leaning over the bulwarks, and a string of them twisted up the mast, feet to woolly pate, as if they had been threaded on a rope fastened to the peak. Only as I swerved at the last instant and flashed past did they slowly twist their heads.

I observed a small group of horsemen on the beach: I supposed it was the only roadway up to Cape York. 'How childish of me expecting to find those sharks still there under the seaplane after alighting.' I had to put my thick woollen scarf round my neck; the sun was burning fiercely – there was no shelter from it in the cockpit, and it was like an oven inside the leather flying helmet.

2.45. The desert shore was very dreary, with not a sign of life for the past hundred miles. I read the magazine – also very dreary: stopped reading to photograph ant-hills; an extraordinary sight; like groups of distant cathedrals standing on points of the foreshore. 'Must be ten feet high, some of them. Photograph will be no good, I fear, as the ant towers are dingy dark brown in colour and their background dingy dull green.'

At 3.20 I saw a house. It faced the sea, high perched in a bay of the hill face; was set in a palm-tree plantation. Somerset mission station, it must be. 'What a joke to think that I had proposed alighting there for petrol. How was I to know? It was the only place marked in capital letters for nearly 400 miles.' I did a whirl-about turn in front of the veranda, vaguely wishing to amuse the occupants who could not have a great deal of amusement in that place, I thought. However, I saw no one.

I left Cape York and headed for Horn Island fourteen miles off. Curiously enough, Thursday Island was not marked on my chart at all. However, the whole group was only twenty miles across so that if I ferreted round behind Horn Island I was bound to find Thursday, I thought.

I recognised it immediately; the passage which it bordered was like a water-field sown with luggers.

Thursday Island. 6 hours 40 minutes, 525 miles. Total 2,002.

## CHAPTER V

### DINNER-PARTY ON THURSDAY ISLAND

I LEFT Thursday Island at 3.16 Greenwich Mean Time (12.46 p.m. local time) for the crossing to New Guinea. This was by my remaining watch, which is particularly accurate and set to Greenwich Mean Time for sextant work. I am going north past Hawkesbury Island to Mulgrave Island and then fifty-one miles across water to Deliverance Island; Deliverance Island to New Guinea, twenty-three miles, and then west along the coast to Merauke – 103 miles. It is not much for the day, but I told myself that I had a lot to attend to this morning, and that as the next place after Merauke is 472 miles on, I had better make an easy day of it. The truth is that nothing would have induced me to miss a night at Merauke if it were only ten miles away.

(Last night picking up Thursday Island was as easy as could be behind Horn Island. I came down near the jetty-head and cast anchor. Quite soon a dinghy put off, with two aboard. The man in the stern-sheets said he was Vidgen; that he was agent for the oil company; that a buoy was ready for me in the lee of the jetty; that he would wait for me at it, throw me a rope and make the seaplane fast. He was cool, calm and efficient, and I took a great fancy to him at once. I hauled in my anchor and stowed it, restarted the motor and taxied slowly against the strong current to within a few feet of where he was holding to the buoy. I switched off, hopped quickly out of the cockpit and caught his rope just before the tide bore the plane out of reach. It was all done in a few seconds without any noise, swearing or fuss; and the seaplane was fast to a proper mooring with a good stout rope. What a pleasant change!

As I bent down, securing the rope, one of my watches slipped out of my breast pocket and, as it sank, it seemed to look at me with mute reproach, its face pale through the green water.

Most of the inhabitants, I would say, came down to the jetty to have a look at me; but I must have come short of expectation, for they soon went away again. Only Australian aborigines continued to drift on to the jetty and off, noiseless, detached, indifferent, impassive. They had hair like thick, black mats, and fascinated me with the absolute blackness of their skins.

While changing the oil, I was badly scared of dropping the sump-plug into the sea; with the result that I soused my bandage in oil. Presently it received a sousing in petrol. This was by no means soothing to the wound, which for some reason still irritated constantly. In the end I took the bandage off and then the finger seemed to bump every object on the seaplane.

Vidgen invited me to stay the night at his place and we motored off, past wooden bungalows almost hidden by the bushy creepers rambling up the veranda posts. The road was reddish, the colour of brick rubble swept from the kilns, and no wonder, for if this is winter, then summer there must be as hot as hell with all the fires full on.)

Abreast Hawkesbury Island.

(After a delicious cold shower I dressed in the one presentable suit I carried in my knapsack. This, I was gratified to find, won a murmur of admiration; though it was not surprising I suppose after the weird rig they had seen me arrive in – dirty old working clothes and dungarees covered in engine oil, dope, paint and dried salt. They had a small party at dinner for a Dutch captain from the Aru Islands, and a Mr. Foxton. I could scarcely believe I was in the same country as my last halting-places. These people were gentle-mannered, and the Dutch style of ceremony used during the evening was a singularly refreshing change. One stood at attention on being introduced and the rule for the evening was punctilious politeness. The Dutchman was like an Englishman, only more handsome than the average, except for his nose, which was meagrely bridged.

Jove! what a dinner that was. They insisted on my having some more beef; I felt capable of dealing with the beef, but what was that compared with the regiment of onions, beans and potatoes around it. However, I was not going to be beaten by the best cooked dish I had tasted for ages; slower and slower I became as each mouthful required more careful stowing; but at last the victory was mine and I was flashing a triumphant beam around the table when what should be marched in but the great great grand father of all apple tarts!)

Mulgrave Island abreast; and my appetite has returned, so now for lunch while *Elijah* starts the fifty-mile water-jump.

(They asked me what I proposed doing in the event of a forced landing among the headhunters. I told them I proposed pouring candle-grease into the cartridge of my .410 double-barrelled pistol, to make the shot a solid bullet. They asked what range it would kill at. 'Ten yards,' I replied. This caused a general laugh, and when I inquired what the joke might be, they said that for one thing I should never see any Papuans, who would keep behind the trees; for another they would not approach so long as I was alive; and thirdly they would twang poisoned arrows at me until they finished me off from 200 yards range or even more. To be quite frank, this had not occurred to me. These natives must be a choice lot; they use arrows barbed both ways. Once the arrow is in you, it is impossible either to push it through or pull it out. Frederick Henry Island, they told me, has plenty of headhunters on it. They come out in canoes and attack any lugger that is becalmed or stopped while making the Princess Marianne Strait. They are purely headhunters, who must have so many heads before they can claim the status of warrior: not cannibals; only those in the interior are cannibal; where meat is scarce. Heavens! what stories they told of a man named Roche. For instance, of his mates being riddled with arrows and of his own escape twice. They said he is a New Zealander who lives on a coconut plantation about eight miles up the Merauke River. I hope I shall meet him.)

The 'plane is very awkward. I rigged the petrol differently, filling the front tank full and leaving the rear tank empty. I thought she might make a better take off with all the weight forward – and I think she did; but the consequence is, she flies nose heavy and I have to write holding the log-book between finger and thumb, the other fingers round the control-stick. Land–o dead ahead – it must be Deliverance Island. . . . So I was not out of sight of land for long; yet had that fresh thrill of finding myself alone with nothing but sea in every direction.

The 'plane is much slower to-day. About 6 m.p.h. I wonder why? Hope the wing surface is not losing tautness and deteriorating, as everyone said it would do in the tropics. Perhaps it is the nose-heavy rigging.

(I surprised Vidgen last night by asking for a blanket to sleep under. The weight seems to keep my nerves quiet. At any rate I slept sound and solid from 9.30 till 7.30. And either because of that, or perhaps with the addition of an easy morning, I feel as fit as a stag. Give me nine hours sound sleep every night and I feel I could accomplish anything. I believe I am going to enjoy this flight after all.)

Nearly up to the Island. It is an atoll with smooth water inside the ring. I can see the reflection of the palms in it from here.

The Island looked like a fragment of paradise. The ring of land was covered with thick jungle, very like the New Zealand bush in appearance – heavy green and dense. But I could see the addition of banana plants with their broad blades, and the nodding heads of palm craning above the rest. It had a rim of pearly white sand, and the whole set on a plateau of dark brown coral just under the surface. Turtle drifted in the water, and flights of fish flitted about with nervous changes of direction. Splodges of magnificent deep purple relieved the dull coral. In such a spot must Adam and Eve have lolled and lazed, splashing about that warm secluded water, and picking their food from easy trees as they needed it. No other land in sight anywhere. Rain clouds gathering.

(Vidgen told me that de Pinedo had alighted there, and subsequently spent hours dashing about the channel in vain efforts to get unstuck, before at last he took to the air again. Asked him where de Pinedo flew to from Thursday Island, but he did not know. Is it possible I am not the first man to fly over this route after all? Not that I should worry about it; I suppose it is quite a different enterprise for a big flying-boat with a crew. As Thursday Island was the last of Australia, I told Vidgen and some others I would carry as much mail as they liked to send, provided I were given some of the letters carried. They busied themselves about the matter, and now I have 145 letters for Japan and other countries before England, besides Roche's mail which I carry to Merauke for him.)

No land in sight yet; surely I have not missed the largest island in the world, 1,600 miles long, when aiming for the middle of it? Out in deep water, miles from anywhere, I saw a green turtle; its flippers steadily flipping. Its course, I noticed, was west by north; but there is no land in that direction for 700 miles – I hope its compass has been properly swung!

(There was a little wooden bank building on Thursday Island and I walked through the heated air to it full of hope. But no money had come for me, and I had to leave with only £18 to see me through to Manila. I suppose it will turn out all right; and petrol might be cheap from now on, since the East Indies is where it comes from.)

Confound it! Land should be in sight by now.

(Someone at Thursday Island had had a lugger stolen, and I was asked to keep an eye open for it. I said I should guess that none of them had ever tried to distinguish a stolen lugger from a 'plane. Oh, surely! surely! they said, that would be quite simple, and to help me they would supply a photograph of it. Presently they brought one; they were sorry, they explained, that they had no photograph of the actual lugger, but here was one of a similar boat. I could easily recognise the stolen craft, because it had a mast two feet shorter. Heavens! what do they take me for? A magician?

Vidgen is a pearl merchant and his office was piled high with shell in one corner. He lent me his car so that I could drive myself back to his house: it was a strange sensation – driving it; I handled it delicately, and every bump to its chassis or sudden jerk of engine speed lacerated my feelings.

In pumping the float bilges I fumbled a bilge-pipe screw-top. Down it sank to the depths. I replaced it as best I could – with a cork. Pleased with the substitute, I then replaced the oil-level indicator-rod with a piece of wire through another cork. Ought I to lay in a supply of corks?)

Jupiter! there is that infernal land right under my nose. Dead flat like a patch of dull mud-tinged water. I had seen it for some time, but thought it a cloud shadow.

Made land 2.12. Jerai Bay, I think. Dead flat marsh as far as I can see in any direction. Look at the crocodiles! Father croc, mother croc and all the little crocs – going across the mud as if hell itself were at their tails. Heavens! see that one. It must be fifteen feet long, lashing its tail with great writhing strokes till I can fancy the tip cracking like a whip. Sheets of liquid mud spraying into the air now from this side, now from the other. Hideous, terrifying, prehistoric monsters! Well, for once the fear of God is in them. Curious how differently the 'plane affects creatures. What scores there are! I wonder if I could secure a photograph. No! useless – they are the same colour as the mud.

I have not located my position yet. A river. Moorhead River? No, impossible, because this empties into a bay, whereas the chart shows Moorhead to empty at a point. It looks to me more like Jerai Bay. Did I make a landfall east of Jerai Bay? No, impossible; besides, the chart shows no river in Jerai Bay. I must keep my eye skinned. This land is all exactly alike. And I have no idea what to expect for Merauke. I do not want to miss it.

Abreast of river 2.26.

2.36, fish-trap like an arrow headed out to sea with very long barbs on either side. Some natives. Black burnt patches. Vast flat plains inland, that resemble unlimited pasture of dark green grass – swamp, really, I suppose. I have not located position yet. The coast bears 310° magnetic; therefore I must be past Bensbach River. Yet there has been no sign of it. Something queer about this, I think.

2.45, smoke – five miles ahead. 2.48, sand beach. Suddenly noticed the lid of the locker behind me had flown open. With back-stretched arm I managed to shut it. Hope everything has not fallen out. Thank heaven I put the bilge pump in the front cockpit. A boat with masts on the beach; it looks like that stolen lugger; and a man is building a civilised-looking hut alongside it, too: very suspicious; just the sort of place where I should try to hide a stolen lugger if I thought the natives safe. 2.53, coconut plantation. Village, natives. That must be Mariu, twenty miles from Merauke. Shall I shoot up Roche's house before alighting? Wind S.S.E. Have written thirteen pages during the crossing. It makes a difference – feeling fit. Merauke, 3.10.

2 hours 24 minutes. 212 miles. Total 2,214.

## CHAPTER VI

### A TOWN OF MUD

'LEFT Merauke 10.55 G.M.T. (10.55 + 9.20 = 8.15 local time). Wet through with heat. I cut it too fine altogether at Merauke. I knew the floats must touch the scrub-tops. I waited for her to trip and crash. . . . Hot! . . .'

Merauke was a place criss-crossed with roadways, a compact settlement in a clearing carved from the thick profusion of tropical growth surrounding it. The river flowed before it, wide, flat and muddy. As soon as I flew overhead, I could see the place pouring natives on to the jetty and river-banks. Before I had made one circuit, I could pick out figures in white embarking in a launch; so gave up the idea of flying up-river to Roche's plantation. Studying the layout of the river I presently picked out the bright tricolour of a Dutch flag nodding from a drum-buoy. I made a bad alighting – how depressing and annoying it is to fly badly! I was concentrating on the surface, because at the last moment I feared I was not coming down dead into wind and might have some drift. As a result I bumped hard on the surface – perhaps it was not really a hard bump, but one becomes infernally sensitive about it in a seaplane.

The river-bank and jetty were packed tight with natives – Papuans, perhaps 2,000 of them. Many wore only a conch shell for trousers. All the five white men were there too. Three of them were missionaries with long beards straggling to the waist. They seemed childishly glad to see a stranger; but none could speak English or French, which surprised me. The gesaghebber and the doctor had a smattering of English; but it was terribly exhausting work trying to make myself understood, and trying to understand them. Roche had left for Daru by launch three days before, so that my bringing his mail was useless.

The gesaghebber told me that de Pinedo had flown over (eight years before) without alighting; had made Dobbo in the Aru Islands. It seems queer how we both chose the same places, though I dare say natural enough if properly considered. Other things he told me were: that he himself had shot a crocodile eighteen feet long and all the natives for miles had come for a feast of it; and that I ought to sight the monthly K.P.M. steamer 600 miles west – somewhere near Ambon. I had to buy petrol from a Chinese storekeeper and, to my disgust, pay 4s. a gallon for it. I worked out the very least amount I dared set out with for Dobbo, and I refuelled with that as soon as I could after alighting. No suitable oil was to be obtained; so it is lucky that my engine uses so little and that I brought along a spare gallon tin. My next concern was for a chart. I had not been able to obtain one in Sydney, and had nothing to cover the sea-hop from New Guinea to the Arus, or the 465-mile flight from the Arus across the Banda Sea to Amboina. I had not worried much about it, feeling sure I should have no trouble in obtaining a chart at Merauke. Now that I saw what Merauke was like I was not surprised to learn that no such thing existed there: and I should have been in a pretty fix had not the gesaghebber owned a map, been a good fellow, and given it to me.

It was now dark and the doctor took me for a walk through the place. The narrow streets, with the flimsy wooden or bamboo structures crowding them, seemed alive, crawling with natives. One or two Chinese stores surprised me with their excellence. I saw some Paradise birds – they were skinned and stuffed with alum, I think. They were the most glorious saffron, yellow, russet and brown shades that I ever saw. I just stood holding my breath, lost in wonder at their magnificence. I had to buy one. I believe they used to cost five pounds each before they were declared contraband in every country to prevent extermination of the species. Mine cost me less than a gallon of petrol. I packed it as carefully as I could in grease-proof paper, taking all possible care of the two tail plumes; these were more like two strong hairs two feet long. Yet the bird was no larger in body than a thrush.

The doctor then showed me his hospital. It consisted of a narrow belt of stone-floored building which bounded the four sides of a large open square. The natives remain in the open when sick, and each squatted chattering beside his or her own little fire. So that dozens of these fires flickered in the square. The doctor was sorry I had not arrived a day sooner; he could have shown me his albino, but unfortunately the patient had died that morning. The natives are mostly rotten with sex disease. I wondered if they had suffered from that when purely cannibal and before being touched by civilisation; I could not make myself well enough understood to find out. The gesaghebber told me later that whenever a native is married all the men of his kampong and any visitors embrace the new wife before the husband.

I was now deposited in the pasan grahan of stone floor and bare walls. This is the local hotel where one may stay for a small charge, but must buy or produce one's own food. I tried to discuss the question of food, but the language at our joint command was unequal to it, so I gave up the attempt and sat in philosophic if solitary state, waiting to see what would happen. Presently a meal arrived to which I did full justice. I had a notion that either the doctor or the gesaghebber sent it, but could not find out. However, I said 'beer'! to the native dressed in a sarong (a Malay, I suppose) who brought the food, and he presently produced a bottle. What a wonderful word, 'beer'; there are not many countries in which that is not understood! And if it should fail, one has only to lift a cupped hand to one's mouth, cock the head back and subsequently smack the lips a few times to obtain something like it. Afterwards I sat and contemplated. It is not lonely in the pasan grahan of bare stone floor and walls, provided no other human beings are there. The black tropical night is outside, and the moths flutter round the hard petrol light. The gecko keeps one company, scuttling over walls and ceiling, making sudden darts at some huge beetle twice the size of itself. One watches the battle with intense interest, the wild rush, the sharp short scuffle until either the lizard glides off with its prey between its jaws or both fall with a floppy smack to the floor and the beetle escapes. In some places I notice the gecko is much more daring than in others; in some parts he is positively timid. Does he assume the character of the householder? The gesaghebber told me that the correct name is tjic-tjac (which is really the little squeaky call he makes to his friend behind the shutter); the 'gecko' is a much bigger lizard living out of doors and calling 'gecko! gecko! gecko!'

When the native came to clear away I set about obtaining a blanket. I lay on the bed, pulled an imaginary blanket over me and then repeated the act with my coat. This produced a piece of material as large as a hand-towel with black and white stripes. There was nothing else on the bed but two pillows and the long bolster or Dutch wife. There was a mosquito-net canopy. I put out the light and tried to sleep. Apart from my twitching, and being itchy and on the jump, there was a prison just behind the pasan grahan. Apparently it was guarded by four native sentries and at every quarter-hour they all sounded bells, one sentry after the other, like cocks picking up the challenge in each other's crow. To judge by the effect it had on me, I should say it was an excellent way to prevent their sleeping for long while at their posts. At about two o'clock I rose, put on woollen underclothes and thick socks, and eventually went to sleep with one pillow on top of my head and the other below.

Next morning I saw the prisoners going off to work

on the roads and was greatly taken with their hearty good-natured expression. There were two husky fellows especially, with beaming faces, laughing away and firing off that rapid, interminable native chatter at each other as they padded along the road. The gesaghebber drew my attention to them. Ideal husbands, I should have thought. He said they were hillmen who had formed the habit of coming to 'town' periodically. There they picked out a succulent-looking town-boy, treated him to a meal of drugged sago, and then carried him back to the hills where they cooked and ate him. The gesaghebber said it was no use hanging them for doing what they considered the correct thing, so they were put on to road-making for a few years – a life they rather liked (the gesaghebber declared) because it entailed regular food without any trouble in obtaining it. There was also a fine strapping young maiden in the gang with a jolly, flashing smile; she was sixteen and had killed her husband with a knife between the ribs. I was extremely pleased to meet two cannibals and a murderess; and as I saw them having a good look at me, too, through the corner of their eye, I hope the pleasure was mutual.

Both the Dutchmen had wives with them. The doctor's was quite a new one. She turned up on the jetty in the morning and was singularly attractive from a male point of view. She was charming. I think one would have placed her as a Dutch woman anywhere, with her light honey-coloured hair. I noticed they did not invite me to their houses; I look pretty rough in my seaplane kit, I suppose.

The word Merauke should mean mud. The flat, flowing river was muddy, the banks were mud; the low-lying country all round put one in mind of sloppy mud, as did also the reeds, the willow-like scrub and the swamp grass.

I taxied down river to the far side and headed back into the slight easterly breeze. The air was hot and sticky, the water surface tired. The 'plane failed to rise. I turned and it seemed to take an age to taxi a mile or perhaps a mile and a half down river again. And it was no good, although I held on until nearly into the bank at the river bend. I stopped the motor and let it cool while the 'plane drifted slowly. The heat of the motor met my face. I know nothing that settles despair to the depths of one's heart so much as failing to take off. Why it should do so, I cannot conceive. My project seemed a terribly futile thing, trying to fly round the world in a ridiculous little seaplane, totally inadequate. I drifted in dreary silence, with the heat irritating and fitting me like clothes of hair, and later I taxied further down till I was over by the reeds straggling in the muddy water.

I must have had two miles of clear river ahead of me then. The seaplane seemed to climb out of the water till on the step, when by all the rules she ought to have come away with ease; but as soon as I tried to stroke her off I could feel the suction of the smooth water pull at the float heels and slow her down. Then, time after time, I pig-jumped her off with a jerk, but she would not keep in the air and settled back. Yet she was nearly off. But now the bank in front was rushing up fast. At the previous run I had noticed how very nearly the seaplane was to taking off close to the bank.[1]

I had no right to go another inch, and I knew it; if I pig-jumped her once more and she failed to keep the air, it was a crash. Some desperate feeling drives one. I held her down to the last few yards, then pulled her off sharply. She jumped the bank. I had been concentrated on the bank; I looked up to find a clump of low trees filling the space in front and to the left. Obviously I could not get over them. I could not turn to the left where the river ran before the trees. I could force the seaplane down to the mud and willowy scrub beneath me, with probable safety to myself but certain destruction to the 'plane. I could not do that. I was already in a skidding turn to the right. Small-leaved shrubs like willows came at me; I had not clearance enough above them to bank properly, and the seaplane skidded towards the trees. If only the 'plane did not feel so infernally heavy in the air. The slots were hanging out: the 'plane had scarcely flying speed. I watched the willow tops under the right wing tip, banking as much as I dared without the wing tip touching. I was aware of the willows under the float; it must touch, but so long as no stump in the small branches caught it. . . . It was the skid I feared. Underbanked, she was skidding to the left. The trees were there. I could not look up from the willows under the right wing tip. I felt as if I were an animal looking away while waiting to be shot. What ages I waited while life stood still!

[1] It may have been shallow there and the float-heels picking up the recoil of the bow-waves from the bottom.

No crash. I must be round.... Coconut-trees ahead. I jumped above their tops and skimmed them, gathering speed. It was like flying a mud-clogged old wheelbarrow with wings. Before I left that sea of tufted coconut-tops I suddenly felt sick to death of them.

# CHAPTER VII

## STRANGE COUNTRY, STRANGE PEOPLE

I WAS flying along the coast of New Guinea. The native villages or kampongs each consisted of a double row of huts in a long clearing with tall solid bush on three sides and the long sloping beach on the fourth. The sand ran out shallow for a long way so that the breakers resembled white scratches between the wide ribbons of flat water stretching along the coast. Usually there were hundreds of natives dotting the beach in front of each kampong, and they bolted for their lives in every direction. Some in outrigger canoes in the shallows jumped out and tore through the water making nearly as much splash as the crocodiles had done. Sometimes they stopped, turned, looked up, and then went off again as if the very devil were after them with red-hot tongs. In some kampongs they peered round the corner of their huts; while in others they just stood wherever they happened to be, whether on the shore or in the way between the rows of huts, and stared up at the 'plane without movement. But in every kampong, whatever they might do, they did it all as one man, I noticed. I wish I could have listened to the discussions in those kampong councils during the next few days.

I was going to fly right across Frederick Henry Island; I could not resist the temptation; and was quite excited. According to the gesaghebber there were some kampongs of good natives on the edge of Princess Marianne Strait (which separates island and mainland) but inland only headhunters, and no white man had penetrated there. Now I was flying over the mainland making for the strait. Great blotchy cloud-shadows slid over the ground below at twenty miles an hour, in the same direction as the 'plane's shadow; its pace was uncanny as it flitted over heavy bush-tops, across light green swamp grass or tall reeds waving like corn, meeting a wall of forest trees and skimming up it almost too quickly for the eye to follow.

I flew over a steely bright riband of river, coiling its way deep in heavy forest. The air was uncomfortable, not with vicious bumps, thank heaven! but with a movement like the bow of a lively steamer pitching into a storm. At every pitch my face was showered with petrol from the air vent in the front tank, and looking up I could see another shower leave the top tank vent like the first steam from a ship's siren. I was surprised to see two kangaroo lolloping over an arid patch of desert land, dotted sparsely with shrub-like trees.

Now I passed over Princess Marianne Strait, a snaky length of grey silver stretching as far as eye could see; I was above Frederick Henry Island. It was flat to look at like a slab, and covered with tall, heavy, impenetrable-looking forest. After skimming this for some distance, deeply interested in the matted tangle of tree-tops, the forest ended suddenly like a cliff, and I was flying over a sea of reeds or tall grass, with the wind-puffs driving across in flattening waves. A storm-cloud, heavy and black-cored, filled the sky to my left. To be caught under that meant a tropical deluge with a visibility of only a few yards; it might be awkward flying low over that sea of swamp with sudden islands of jungle forest rising from it. The uneven following wind continually caused the 'plane to whizz downwards and dart upwards. I strained my eyes for a sight of the headhunters. Occasionally I caught a glimmer of water in the reeds. It must bc a vast swamp. There was something horrible about it, as about a quicksand. It would probably be soft enough to dump the 'plane in without hurt to me, if the engine failed; but once in it I should be worse off than in the wildest of oceans; besides the morass and the headhunters around it, it must be teeming with crocodiles, though I could not see any.

Then, under me, the swamp took on a definite pattern. I could scarcely believe my eyes. But there was no doubt about it; the land was striped with a pattern that stretched for miles. As though it had been drained by straight ditches and the soil heaped on the long strips between, and now was all covered in reeds. It must be due to some simple natural cause, I was thinking, when I was astonished to notice deeper drains crossing the first at right angles or nearly so, every few hundred yards, as if to draw off the water from the lesser drains. And others, largest of all, like little canals, to tap those. Well, it could not be man's work because there was no trace of man anywhere; it must be a delusion caused by some peculiarity in the reed-growth. Next instant I came upon a small elongated patch of cleared ground in the middle of the waving reed. It looked like a patch of mud in a light-green sea; but it proved that the striped pattern was caused by drains – for it straddled one, about six feet deep, with water in the bottom, or it might have been liquid mud. The cleared sides were irregularly spattered with a few young banana plants. Head-hunters! But where were they? where did they live? why cultivate the middle of a swamp? And how did they get through it? I saw two more planted patches, one having water dammed up in the ditch. I was holding my camera ready and photographed it. Further on there was a seemingly drier spot with shorter grass and on this I saw a primitive, man-made shelter, a flimsy palm-leaf or reed-thatch barely supported by four thin leggy sticks. But, search as I might, I could not see a native anywhere.

At 9.58 (local time) I flew over the sea again. It had taken thirty-nine minutes to cross the island. I must make reasonably accurate navigation of the 260-mile sea-hop now begun; for, though the Aru Islands were a good target, the Dutch map was rough to navigate by. North was not marked on it – nor the magnetic variation; also I did not know my compass deviation. However, the position of the Arus relative to New Guinea was likely to be correct. Therefore I had flown on a steady compass course until over the island, before attempting any correction. I then observed my error, and finding myself to be 14° off my course, thus determined by a single observation the combined errors were due to drift, variation, deviation and incorrect map-orientation. As a result I changed course 14° – from 294° to 280°.

How safe and friendly the sea felt after that island! I became hungry, ate a meal and then sat musing or writing. What was the meaning of the pattern in the swamp? An old civilisation? It could only be due to man, with that peculiar regularity; a vast labour it must have been. . . . I changed course 30° to port for four minutes to avoid a rain squall. The drift was less now, so that I should be borne a little south of my mark unless I changed course; but perhaps that would not be a bad thing. A grand south-easter was bowling me along in great style. '11.40, fine weather. 12.0, the sun on my neck broiling hot. . . . What a nuisance, not getting off this morning; evidently due to that tropical difficulty they talked of; I only had on about forty gallons, too. . . . 12.10, I ought to pick up land soon.' However simple the water-jump might be, one became uneasy when the time for seeing land approached – one *might* have read off, or set down, a bearing incorrectly, and be flying nowhere near the objective. '12.13, land–o? Yes, no, yes, no; 12.14, no; 12.15, well, that looks like land. . . . But I can see the muddy sea behind it, so that's no good. 12.16, it was a cloud shadow. Wind veering to south slightly. 12.19, looks very like land ahead. Penamboelai, I think. Three cheers! Mainland in rain, I fear.'

Every time I made a note when trying to determine position, I looked up from the log with a fresh eye; whereas, if I stared continuously at an object I hoped was land, it would assume the most fantastic shapes.

At 12.43 I entered the channel between the main

islands Wokam and Kobroor; it seemed to be full of war-canoes with high stem, and stern-posts; some scuttled over the water, furiously paddled. On either side of the passage were magnificent, tall forest trees, from which dangled lianas like black ropes, while their tops were festooned with pink, rose and red creepers. Next moment a frightful bump drove all thought of beauty from my mind and I hurriedly fumbled to secure my belt before I should be tossed out. . . .

Dobbo, 1.25. 5 hours 10 minutes; 472 miles. Total 2,686.

Dobbo was an island facing big Wokam across a narrow passage. The water I came down on was a deep, sparkling blue. Jetties and jumbled wooden shanties encroached upon it along the water-front. At the back of these the island was a field of palms with wind-blown crests. The first thing I did on coming to rest was to drop my goggles overboard; the draw-wire interlocking the two halves of the front cockpit cover soon followed; so I carefully climbed back into the cockpit before handling my camera; my touch must be awry. Four Englishmen or Australians put off in a launch, which chugged round and round the seaplane. To hear English again made me feel like a boy home from school. They shouted remarks and jokes; but, every time I suggested their coming up close, they seemed to become deaf. At the time, this puzzled me. Presently I saw a launch, flying the Dutch black, red and white, bearing down on the seaplane. The gesaghebber was interesting: he appeared youngish and had a short, quick manner of speaking; as if using brief sentences for a sign of efficiency. He wore spectacles with those steel rims that become discoloured by rust; and had a restless, bird-like, almost fussy, air which made me think he was a non-smoker; but it may have been the sense of his responsibility as the man with complete local power, allowing him no rest. I should say that once he had dug himself into the idea of efficiency nothing could dislodge him from it. I felt sure he would rise several steps in the government service in the course of time. I noticed that he was always exceedingly polite to the Australians and spoke to me through them as if they were a kind of speaking tube. *Elijah* was towed to the big drum-buoy flying the Dutch flag and made fast. Then I was taken ashore in the government launch to pick up my petrol. There was a tremendous press of natives on the jetty, thousands of them, and they suddenly burst into a shout that would have raised the roof of the sky. It is inevitably thrilling to hear a great crowd shouting as one man – even if embarrassing. On the jetty, the gesaghebber proudly showed me the fuel he had had the kindness, the foresight and the efficiency to prepare for me. I found a formidable array of big drums rolled up side by side on the jetty; their weight must have amounted to five times that of my whole machine; unfortunately they were of crude oil instead of petrol.

One Australian pearler had his wife there, and children, too. They looked pale and delicate; and I thought how difficult it must be to bring up children in such a moist, sticky heat that must make even grown-ups petulant.

I spent a wonderful evening among the bachelors. There were three, all pearlers, Australian and English, and they lived together in an airy ramshackle old structure of two stories, with wide verandas and hanging rattan curtains instead of doors. It is curious how, when men are together, they seem to loosen up and, however much they may be hoodwinking each other in reality, seem to talk quite without reserve.

They told me that the natives of Frederick Henry Island were the worst in New Guinea and related various stories of luggers being attacked by them in Princess Marianne Strait. They were most interested to hear about my trouble in locating position on the coast of New Guinea and of my finding only one river there instead of two; because there had been a much-discussed long-prevalent doubt as to whether there were any Bensback River at all. The river I *had* found they said was Java Creek; and that it was there that Roche's partner had been killed.

They also told me a story about Deliverance Island, the little palm-covered atoll in the middle of Torres Strait, which I had thought so beautiful. One of them sheltered on it for several days when crossing the strait. They said that a man once went there to hunt turtle. When he reached the island, he decided to remain; and did so, a solitary hermit, for twenty years, eating so much turtle that he perspired turtle and you could smell him turtley yards away. During one period at the time of the War, he saw no human being for three years, and when a pearler at last called, the first question the hermit asked was 'had he seen B— lately?' 'Why?' 'Because, the last time B— called at the island, he had promised the hermit a belt.' B— had been dead five years.

I managed to borrow a rug that night and slept like the dead from 9.30 till 5.30. Sound sleep was the whole secret of this flying game. Without a good sleep after a long day of seaplane labour, it was like having a thousand prickly devils under the skin. At Dobbo I had escaped the fatigue of trying for several hours to make myself understood in nursery English.

The pearlers asked me to take them for a flight in *Elijah* and offered to pay me for it. I refused but afterwards felt guilty for doing so – if they wanted a flight, I should have given them one; and yet I think I was right in refusing; the Dutch were so punctilious; they expected an airman to say at what hour he would arrive, and then to arrive at that hour. As the clock struck they would be waiting for him in a launch. They would treat him with the utmost courteous ceremony, and do everything they could to make his stay a successful one, but they expected him to arrive on time to the minute.

When the pearlers came to see me off, a Malay prince and his princess were there. The prince was small, delicate-looking and quiet; an aristocratic remnant of some very old, once highly-civilised nation – standing there among some of its rough barbarian conquerors. I felt that I ought to behave. His complexion was quite pale, more like that of a Siamese than a Malay; and he wore the best cut white flannels that I saw on the island – in fact, I should not be surprised if they came from Savile Row. His wife was perfectly charming; with her tiny feet and hands, her little figure so delicately formed; her flesh firm and cool, delicious to look at; her wishful-to-please smile and the flash of small white teeth; her face was not dark, but a pale brown which might have been that of a European but for the black hair and slightly Oriental slant of eye. Her chief attraction, of course, was her being utterly, completely woman from toes to finger-tips. . . .

. . . . . . . . .

My first water-jump of 80 miles to the Kei Islands and the second of 110 miles to Kasioei Island were uneventful except that, when I came to pump petrol from the bottom to the top tank, I found I had stuck to my seat. A tube of seccotine in my knapsack had burst and spilt over the trousers I put on at Dobbo. It had appeared to be quite firmly set, but evidently the tropical heat, or mine, had proved too much for it. I had to prise myself loose very gingerly, not wanting to arrive with seatless trousers at Amboina, the capital of the southern spice islands and of this end of the Dutch East Indies.

Many of the islands in the Watoebela group were not shown on my map. Of course the little ones would not be needed on a small-scale political map. But anything that sticks out of the sea is an island to an airman, and its absence from the map makes it difficult to determine position. Watoebela itself was the ideal tropical island of fiction; dazzling white surf beating at a ring of bleached atoll-sand; dark green jungle-trees on the land with palms predominant, their crests streaming before the wind; a calm lagoon as clear as crystal and yet full of colour – of green in every tint from faint light to deep dark; of blues from azure to the sparkling purple of the outer ocean; but the remarkable feature was that every colour, no matter what, looked utterly pure and transparent. There seemed to be hundreds of islands, many uninhabited, some with kampongs half hidden in dense forest where one building always stood out from the rest; a mosque, I think, with a double pagoda roof – a smaller roof set on top of the other. It was wild and beautiful; and I could not conceive an earthly paradise more lovely.

There were many praus full of natives fishing behind the reefs. From one, all on board dived into the sea; they must have taken me for a devil; and a devilish spirit immediately entered me; I began flying straight at them, close to the surface, and jumping the prau at the last moment. Some paddled madly for a few yards and then stopped dead, some stared open-mouthed, others crouched in the prau. I think it was a shame, scaring the poor unfortunate natives; but I continued to enjoy myself uproariously doing it, and watched with childish glee when a whole beachful of them scattered as if their party had been exploded. . . . Yet, heavens! down on the surface it was like the glaring heat of a furnace.

I was just thinking I should weep if I lost the lovely trade-wind bowling me along, when the engine's throbbing roar subtly changed in note and I knew by its increased 'bite' that the wind was dropping. A few minutes later, on reaching the east end of Ceram, the heavens opened and emptied. Land and sea were blotted out and the only visibility was within a small sphere about the 'plane, like that of a lamp in a grey, wintry twilight. I was kept in continual suspense waiting for the headlands to loom up suddenly. The sea below was a leaden grey, seething with the heavy drops, and at a few yards' distance, impossible to distinguish from the rain itself. I flew into squall after squall, no sooner drawing a deep breath in relief at emerging from one than holding it again on entering another. The downpour chilled me to the bone, and I did not have time to log changes of course and wind, but could only jot them down on the map. Before I reached Amboina I was dead tired, and I was heartily glad to see the island. I barely noticed, as I climbed over the saddle, that the land below was crowded and heavily cultivated, the first piece of tame country I had seen since I left Sydney. It looked depressingly dull, its colour a bilious green.

Amboina 2.30; 5 hours 28 minutes. 465 miles. Total 3,151.

## CHAPTER VIII

### CONTRASTS AT AMBOINA

A NUMBER of officials put off to the seaplane in a launch. They were in smart white uniforms, and I wished I had one of my own, or, better still, one like theirs which would mask my identity; my old flying clothes made me feel aggressive and garish amongst them; and in the suave atmosphere of orderly officialdom it seemed a menial labour, obtaining petrol, then refuelling with it gallon after gallon, while precariously perched on the slippery floats or engine cowling, and sousing oneself in the process.

There was something unreal about Amboina. I felt I could have squeezed water from the listless, languid air. Vague, dark-grey clouds sagged until they met the land or the sea, discharged in big pelting drops, then slowly lifted until absorbed again by the dull overcast sky above. In fact, though I had left the Aru Islands that morning in the middle of the dry, I had reached Amboina in the middle of the rainy, season.

And the way civilisation rubbed shoulders with savagery made Amboina unreal. Modern concrete wharves, without even a crack in them, not far from dark old palm-thatched native huts. Diesel-engined steamers and motor-launches pushing through a host, of long, thin-gutted praus that seemed to defy every law of safety, balance and seaworthiness. A bare-footed native padding along the street with enormous panniers of fruit balanced at either end of a long bamboo pole, like the scales of Father Time, the ends springing up and down in tune with his jog-trot; beside him a native in respectable white ducks; flitting past them both a uniformed civil servant peddling his bicycle. There were wide streets with a stream conducted in a stone gutter beside the pavement. Houses of stone, each set back in its garden. Motor-cars.

I found myself in the care of a young hulpgesaghebber, and in the evening was taken to interview the Resident of Amboina, who governs the Southern Moluccas, an area equal to about twice that of Great Britain, I think. He was a large and heavily-built man with big weals across his face which I took to be sword cuts. Whether handsome or not, I could not decide, but his manner was powerfully impressive. I was intensely curious to know what was going on behind those stern, commanding features and I tried to tempt him into the open with the story of what I had seen on Frederick Henry Island. I suggested that the island had once been thickly inhabited, that the workings of the land were evidence of some past unknown civilisation. But either he was not interested or pretended not to be; and, although he clapped his hands and ordered the Malay boy to fetch whisky and cigars, I felt as though I were up before the headmaster for breaking bounds, and only spared a caning because of special instructions to treat me softly. I did my best to thank him for the exceptionally efficient and kind treatment I had received, for the moorings prepared and for official assistance everywhere I had alighted. All this, I learnt, had been ordered by the Governor-General, who was the Amboina Resident's only superior in the East Indies.

The hulpgesaghebber invited me to stay at his house and I gladly accepted; I think he did it out of pure kindness. This was the first time I had been invited to stay with a Dutchman. He seemed to worry about it all the time I was there. Of course he was keeping a zealous eye on me, but would it be thought he was fraternising too readily with a foreigner, or did his deeply ingrained domesticity make him feel guilty of loading more work on a young wife with children to look after? I found it difficult to fathom this Dutchman. Outwardly he was like an Englishman, only much more handsome, more efficient, more serious – it is true he would laugh and joke, but with an almost mathematical precision, and even then would suddenly withdraw and wear an air of impenetrable reserve as if he had some secret despair, or had had a sudden attack of doubt whether ambition alone were sufficient to live for. I found no sign of his taking the slightest personal interest in me; I think he regarded me as one might regard a plate – to be passed on to the next man, with perfect manners of course, as soon as possible.

All through the evening the clouds dropped on the place, discharged their load of rain and lifted; towards night the downpour left a false chill in the air, which entered one's body like a warning of fever; and there was a reek of damp and decay, an absence of the faintest stir of air which made one conscious of an exotic atmosphere.

In the morning I looked every few minutes at a giant banana plant across the road from the hulpgesaghebber's house; it had a cluster of broad blades as tall as a man and I could not detect the slightest sway of one tip. I was already thinking of a take off with despair when my host informed me that they *never* had any wind there. So not only would my seaplane never take off; but, water-logged in the moist heat, it would rot. . . .

I found *Elijah* guarded by a native policeman camped in a dinghy. Dozens of praus, motionless and silent, full of natives, men, women and children, their paddles suspended above the surface, were drawn round in a circle while I sweated in the heat to complete the fuelling, change plugs, check tappets, stow gear, clothes, ropes, engine-cover, cockpit-covers, propeller covers, and pump all the bilges.

The town was near the end of a long arm of sea which almost cut the island in half. On each side of the inlet a densely forested slope, rising steeply from the water, breathed out steamy mist under the rain-clouds shrouding the top.

I ran the seaplane for a mile and a half, two miles. As well expect a wallowing log to fly, the surface was so calm; so calm that a large prau, sail drooping, reflected a dull, inverted picture of itself as still as an oil painting. 'Perhaps a breeze would come?' I suggested to the hulpgesaghebber, waiting in the launch. 'No, there never was a breeze.' 'But the sailing praus?' 'They were content to drift down with the tide.' I asked the launch to forge ahead of me at full speed so that I might try to bump off its wash. . . .

It was futile to continue, I told the hulpgesaghebber, as he disembarked me. The motor would only break up in the terrific heat generated by moving through the air so slowly at full throttle and with a diminished sump of thinned-out oil.

I must clear my brain and devise some entirely fresh plan; goaded by irritation from the hot-house atmosphere, by a sense of futility and despair, I was only butting against a wall like an angry bull. So that when the hulpgesaghebber suggested motoring to see a native village, I thought it might be a profitable diversion, likely to clear my head and give new ideas a chance to creep in. And, after all, Amboina is historically one of the most interesting places in the world. However, I sounded him first about the cost; it would be the price of six gallons. After that, once started on the road to extravagance, away went four more gallons in cigars.

First, the hulpgesaghebber took me to see how a native lives in his village. Very simply, was my conclusion; he lives on a tree, one tree a year; eats it, drinks it, burns it, or sells it. This is the sago-palm, short, thick, smooth-boled. The native selects his palm for the year, hacks it down, splits it open and with a sharp instrument scratches out the soft centre, which looks like long-fibred sawdust. Apparently it is left with water in a trough made from a sago-palm shell, until it goes bad, when the fibre is squeezed dry, and the residue left in another trough until it has gone bad again; finally the fermented paste is made into sago bread, sago pudding, sago soup, or sago cakes. (It shows the educational advantages of travel; because I always thought the hateful dish known at school as 'frog's eggs' was made with grain like rice.) The used-up fibre is thrown out – there was a kind of morass of it under the standing trees and we crossed it on slippery planks.

Next we drove round wooded headlands along a twisty, narrow, high-perched road. At another village we clambered down from the road to a hut. Except that it was more flimsy and had several compartments, I can only compare it with a garden tool-house. It was full of natives chattering, and grunting, with surprise at, or in acceptance of, my guide's explanations. Now the one thing I longed to taste was the notorious durian and, after enough chatter to start a war, one was produced. It had a skin like a prickly crocodile, and was as big as a coconut. I understand that when ripe it falls without warning, and that where possible the natives avoid sleeping under the tree. Its taste was perfect, but difficult to describe, creamy, rich, smooth, piquant; nectar could not be more delicious. 'Passion fruit', it should have been named; it had a provocative, tempting flavour, almost irresistible; and was apt to stink in one's nostrils at odd moments afterwards, just when one had completely forgotten ever having eaten it. The smell was a compound of rotten eggs and dead dog. I indulged with restraint.

By the time we returned I had come to a decision, firstly to reduce the load, and also to cut down the distance, measures which appeared simple and obvious as soon as I had made up my mind to the great sacrifice they represented. I went through all my gear and left behind whatever I possibly could – clothes, tools, sailing directions, papers, amounting in all to 19lb., or rather more than the weight of 2½ gallons. I decided also to jettison 5 gallons of petrol, which would save 36lb., and leave me with 30 gallons or six hours' fuel.

As for the length of flight, my next port was Menado, where I was due to obtain more oil and where I was expected. I searched for any other port nearer, and decided to make for Ternate. I had considered Ternate before starting the flight, but turned it down because of the open roadstead. However, this Banda Sea appeared to be very calm.

On going to change my last five-pound note but one, I met de Bas, and took an immediate fancy to him. There was something familiar about him, though I could not decide what. He had a kind of bantering, devil-may-care manner, looked as tough as a brazil-nut, with clean-cut features and powerful build. He was manager of a trading company; but, though I have no doubt he made a wonderful business buccaneer, it seemed to me that he was cast in the wrong century. What a grand pirate was lost here – the very devil of a fighter! He invited me to spend the night at his house. I accepted with enthusiasm, and no one could have more keenly anticipated a wild night among the belles of Amboina. I found him alone in a large stone house with lofty rooms, a fine place facing the square, which was planted with tropical shrubs and trees dripping after the downpour. There was an atmosphere of rank growth and decay about the vegetation of Amboina. As we dined, my host seemed to withdraw into melancholy humour as if his previous joviality had only been a veneer to cover a secret tragedy. I began to wonder if there was something about me which induced melancholia in Dutchmen. But I preferred to think it was due to my flying towards Europe and their home country. After dinner, all we did was to talk a while together and then go to bed.

In the morning, he was in splendid form again, and gave me a grand breakfast, bacon and eggs – with rows of eggs. I had been hungry ever since reaching the town; coffee and a roll are no foundation to build an English day on, while lunch was late and dinner so late that it only caused nightmares. De Bas came down 'to watch the fun', as he put it, and brought some of his friends.

To and fro I raced across the water opposite the town. The surface was sprinkled with praus, and each one thinking the plane had singled it out for destruction paddled madly in a different direction to escape. It was a severe strain, with the constant watch for fishing stakes and swerving to avoid praus, with the blasting roar in my ears and the suspense as to whether the motor would break up.

Finally I told the launch I had no hope of taking off there; that my only chance was the open sea and a broken surface; and could they tow one there? The hulpgesaghebber was troubled; it was a long way. Volumes of Dutch were poured out. But in the end we started off with the seaplane in tow – I think de Bas must have jockeyed him into doing it.

De Bas, after observing how close the seaplane had been to taking off from the launch's waves, said it was a pity they could not give me a 'permanent wave' – he roared with laughter at the joke, though I am not so sure the others appreciated it. Five or six miles down the inlet there was a slight swell noticeable. I said I thought it might be sufficient, cast off the tow, and bounced into the air at the second attempt.

## CHAPTER IX

### CROSSING THE LINE

AS soon as I reached the open sea at the mouth of the Amboina inlet I flew into clear bright weather over a sparkling blue sea, and was so pleased at escaping, that I waggled the wings of the seaplane and flipped the elevators to make it switchback; which was premature, for, at Amboina, I had been so obsessed like a monomaniac with the one idea of escaping, that my wits had been blunted to every other consideration. Determined to discard every article I possibly could I had thrown out the map given me by the Dutchman at Merauke. By the time I discovered that I could obtain neither map nor chart at Amboina (the capital of the Moluccas!) it was too late; I had already sent mine away. Therefore I had a 140-mile sea to fly without a map, before I got back on to my own chart. I had not worried in the slightest, but had taken a look at the big map in the Resident's office, read off the bearing of the first land, uninhabited Ombira Island, and told myself that nothing could be more simple than to fly on the one bearing until I reached the island. How could I miss a big island like that? When, therefore, after turning Amboina Island and flying on the northerly bearing for thirteen or fourteen miles, I flew up against the tail of a big island blocking my way and of which I had not the slightest recollection, I was perplexed. I racked my memory but could recall no land at all on the map between Amboina and the island. 'Well,' I thought, 'it can only be some trivial island, too small on the map to notice,' and I flew to the east side of it, which appeared to take me less off my course than the west. I found it was a black looking country with high, densely-forested slopes, and rising several thousand feet, in dark bluish haze; how high I could not tell, because the mountain-tops were hidden in cloud. Waiting every moment for it to come to an end, I seemed to fly on interminably, five, ten, fifteen miles. When I had flown along it for twenty miles and no end in sight yet, I was anxious and astonished. And a few minutes later I was dismayed to see land loom up ahead of me through the haze. When I found that I was impassibly blocked by a massive range of mountains, black and threatening, stretching away to the east as far as I could see with the tops hidden in the clouds, I was astounded. And now I was in a nice fix; returning to try the other side of the land meant using up all my fuel reserve, and, therefore, if I retraced my course to the first point of the land, then I must go right back to Amboina for more fuel; on the other hand I had no idea what height the mountains were, so dared not attempt to cross them flying blind into the clouds. I could see only one course open to me – and began climbing; I would mount to the cloud ceiling, fly along the land beside me up to the head of the bay, and then back, seeking a gap between clouds and mountains;

if I could find none within twenty miles then I must return to that damned Amboina.

As I flew on, slower than ever while the seaplane laboured to gain height, my heart sank. I could never face that dreadful Amboina inlet again. A blind shot at the mountains ahead began to tempt me, and I grew troubled with fear. Then, turning a headland, I found a saddle in the range on my left, with a rain-squall above it. I could not see if there was a passage through under the squall. I opened up the throttle, but the climbing pace seemed deadly slow while I watched the squall feeling for the pass to close it. Suddenly I caught a glimpse of blue water over the saddle, and, turning down the nose of the 'plane, I scuttled for it at full throttle. I was in the fringe of rain. A few seconds and I was over, in the sunlight again.

I had been flying about 20° east of my course along the unknown coast, so now decided to fly 10° west of it until I fetched Ombira. If I did not sight land within two and a half hours of Amboina I would fly due east until I did so. But I had no confidence in myself now and began to feel I might be anywhere. Well, what did it matter? I thought; and then felt ravenous. As I sought for the remains of the excellent jam and egg sandwiches given me at Dobbo, it made my mouth water to think of them. Alas! they had fermented. Next I tried the biscuit tin, only to find the contents saturated with petrol fumes. Some bread I found, its history forgotten; it was mouldy, but I ate it with butter; at least it was preferable to fermented sandwich and petrol biscuit. I longed for a smoke; but my pipe was broken and the cigars were in the front cockpit: the impossibility of reaching them made me realise how desirable they were.

I did not seem to worry properly about my whereabouts; or even care deeply. In due course I sighted Ombira right ahead – to think that I had ever worried at all about finding an island of that size – fifty miles long and twenty-five wide! Why! I could find it with both eyes shut. It was said to be well-watered, fertile and healthy, yet totally uninhabited because the natives declared it haunted. On drawing level, it seemed steep, poor, dull and miserable, and, haunted or not, did not seem desirable land. I had just turned the island when I was startled by a weird and an accountable sight – three black patches on the sea, slowly moving in a row. Everywhere else the sea appeared normal. As I drew nearer I found that actually they were not black, but black and white; each round patch of water, about twenty yards wide, was made of countless white-flecked wave-tongues darting into the air like flying-fish trying to escape, chasing each other round in a tight circle. I could detect nothing extraordinary about the air outside the patches though I flew between two of them; but I assumed that spinning cores of wind were lashing the sea into incipient waterspouts. Their whirl was clockwise.

I found I had only made 155 miles in two hours four minutes – only seventy-four miles an hour with a *favouring* wind. That was terrible. Poor old *Elijah* lumbering on slower every day and with diminishing load. I should never have believed the tropics capable of such an effect – taking off with only thirty gallons. As a landplane, she would have lifted ninety gallons from a large aerodrome. If I lost this wonderful wind which had been favouring me ever since Cairns, I should be in a pretty fix; but, according to the U.S. hydrographic charts (and my faith in their amazing accuracy increased every day) I should have a favouring wind right through to Japan.

I flew up to a wall of rain stretched across from horizon to horizon; but it was only a line squall and I was through in a few seconds. At 2.38 I sighted land again, a group marked 'Five Islands'; instead of five I counted seven, a few acres each and covered with dense pale green scrub. At 3.3 I struck Gilolo, the largest of the Spice Islands after Ceram; but I saw very little sign of habitation along fifty miles of the coast. Tall hills, smothered in dense jungle, rose steeply out of the water. Sometimes the boles of the timber showed up owing to the steepness; but I never saw the ground – always at some height above it the foliage made an impenetrable tangle. Magnificent creepers swarmed over the tree-tops and dangled from them. And the tropical green pervaded everything. Flying at times only a wing-span from the hillside, I disturbed countless snowy white doves, their wings crazily beating the air though they never seemed to get anywhere, and when I looked round it was to see them still vainly beating the same air long after I had passed. Then I saw the Birds of Paradise. And what a difference! 'Handsome duchesses in black coats and with court trains sailing in stately fashion to the quickest possible safety.' They never appeared to hurry, or even to fly; but invariably glided out of sight by the time I drew level. I never caught more than glimpses of a sheeny black spread sailing through the trees. And though I skirted the hillside for miles trying to overtake one of them, they had always, with incomparable grace and ease, glided under cover before I reached them. They were quite different in appearance from the birds I had seen at Merauke, but it never occurred to me for a moment that they could be anything but Birds of Paradise.

I also saw a number of small pale green birds, the same colour all over, as if they had been dipped in it. Shortly after this I logged an entry, 'Rain ahead'. And then the log was a blank.

When I first saw the rain I thought it a joke – that I was just about to cross the *Line* and must expect a ducking. But immediately I shot into it, I was enveloped in a grey dusk and for a brief instant wondered if my time was wrong and I had been caught by the tropical night; after that I thought no more; flying in the obscure light and close to the sea required intense concentration. The water was like a seething grey slab, the waves beaten out flat. Rain poured into the cockpit as if from a roof spout, drove stinging and splashing into my face, ran down my neck and trickled over my body. After a while I seemed to have been flying for ever; and soon I was in a torpor.

When at last I flew out I had difficulty in rousing my brain to thought. It was vaguely fixed in my mind that the squall had lasted for twenty miles. It never occurred to me to work it out exactly from the time. And so I took the two islands in view on my left for Makian and Moti.

Presently, even my dulled wit could not help realising

that only a mile separated the two islands beside me; whereas Makian and Moti according to the chart, should be five miles apart. The only possible conclusion I could reach was that the storm had lasted forty-five miles instead of twenty, and that I was looking at the twin islands Tidore and Ternate. And now that became fixed in my mind – that I was looking at the two islands. Actually, however, I was only looking at *one* island, Tidore, which, like its twin, is purely a volcano rising out of the sea. The whole upper part of it was hidden in dense cloud; in the middle of the island this cloud had poured down the mountain-side like heavy smoke and overflowed on the sea. Thus I took it for two islands, flew to the northern half and looked for the town. Instead, I could find nothing but a deserted coast of dense light-green scrubby jungle. I was bewildered and thought of my remaining hour's petrol supply. Then, rounding a shoulder of the island, I came face to face with another, which, of course, was Ternate. It rose a mile high from a perfect blue sea, without the wisp of a cloud on it, and in bright sunshine. All my troubles cleared and in the twinkling of an eye I was at the northern end of it circling Ternate town.

# CHAPTER X

## NIGHT AT TERNATE

I CIRCLED the town several times, but could not pick up the tricolour on any buoy. Nor could I see any sign of the official launch flying the flag, though certainly the land-edge was packed tight with natives for a mile of its length, as usual.

I could not pick out any buoy at all. All the small craft lying in the roadstead seemed to be tethered to stakes. I alighted downwind of the pier, taxied slowly into the lee of it, and anchored there. Presently, after a commotion among the crowd, the pier disgorged some officials who went down the steps and boarded a launch. I hurriedly collected my shore-going gear on a wing-root before the launch had arrived at the usual distance for me to begin my bawling and frenzied arm-waving. (I was tired; fatigue seemed to rise to my brain and press it against the skull.) In the launch, they were puzzled at first; but stopped, and presently a man in white uniform, quiet and authoritative, seemed to understand what was the matter with me, and ordered a canoe up to the seaplane. This crazy affair, made of a long hollowed-out tree-stem, was so narrow that I could hardly sit in it, and rode so light in the water that I expected at every instant to be dumped in the sea as I crouched precariously at one end, amazed that the native squatting in the other end should be able to keep it upright at all. In the launch I at once began my mooring palaver, now almost automatic: it was not safe for the 'plane to be approached by heavy launches; it must be moored to leeward of the pier, otherwise it would quickly drift among the piles if it broke loose; I needed an anchor of at least fifteen kilos weight (33lb.), a sound rope long enough to bridle both floats (because secured by one float only, the seaplane would swing across wind), and some petrol – not crude oil. . . . It was slow work; no one had much English, and, worse than that, this port was not on the list I had given to the Dutch government. I began to realise what definite orders must have been issued at the other places concerning the seaplane and myself. Here I had no official standing; and found the Dutchmen making up their minds about me, instead of taking me for granted: especially the official of the launch, van Brink, the Assistant Resident, a man with thick, frizzly eyebrows, which in a Scot, so often go with a dry humour and a dry palate; he spoke in a quiet voice as slightly deaf people sometimes do. I thought he must belong to an old family; his authority sat easily on him, and at the same time that he performed a duty he could yet watch what was going on, detached, quizzical; he took a tolerant interest in me, no more; asked me a few personal questions with a careless indifference. His English was terrible and, as he was the only man who could speak any, it was a labour explaining everything.

At first no anchor at all could be found, but in the end two small ones arrived and I joined them together.

One of the other Dutchmen asked me, through van Brink how long it had taken to fly from Ambon, and seemed keen for the time to be as short as possible; it made him feel nearer to it, I suppose. . . .

Well, Dutchmen might appear incurious about my past or future – except for asking *why* I was making the flight – they might not care a brass button to know my views on 'how long bathing-suits should be worn'; but they did want to know exactly to the minute when I was leaving again. Van Brink even wanted to know whether I was going on to Menado or Manila that afternoon – with about an hour's daylight left.

The Captain of Police now conducted me to the hotel, with a thousand yelling native boys jostling at our heels. He knew about five words of English; and at the hotel, where he seemed to dump me hurriedly, no one could speak one word of it. Neither to hear the roar of the motor, nor be teased by incessant questions, was a relief, but a strange one like the solitariness of relief when an aching tooth had been pulled out. I did not fancy my chances of a blanket; they must have thought me queer, wanting one with a night temperature of 80°; these Dutchmen appeared to sleep naked. I sat at a table on the stone-fronted veranda; in the dark room behind me I could hear tjic-tjic, tjic-tjac from the house lizards. The tropical night was strange and soft. Through the veranda-frame of tangled creeper, I could sense the presence outside of broad-leaved, sappy plants; and could fancy their growing measurably all the while – with the sort of rank growth that, if one's body lay in the jungle, would scrawl over it and twine round it in a night. . . .

In the morning the Captain of Police came to fetch me, and I found M. van Brink, he of the eyebrows, waiting for me among the crowd on the pier. My oil was now so low that something must be added to it and I bought motor-car oil. A four-gallon tin had to be broached by the Arab merchant. (There were many Arabs in the Indies; but, somehow, every time I met an Arab out of Arabia it seemed wrong.) This Arab demanded that I should pay for the whole tin though I only needed a quarter of it; and there we argued in the grilling sunshine, hemmed in by tightly-packed, jostling, jabbering natives, in a little circle with the tin between us on the tar-oozing pier-deck. I could tell that van Brink was cocking an eye at my stinginess – I had been tight-fisted about everything – and I hated it; but only dug my toes in more obstinately and put up with the hot spread under my skin as well as I could. Van Brink asked me to send him a telegram from the Philippine Islands to say that I had arrived safely. I made every excuse I could think of – and rightly, as it turned out – but he insisted, until at last I promised; I am ashamed to say I failed to keep my word.

# CHAPTER XI

## PUSS-IN-BOOTS

I HAD thirty-five gallons on board – five gallons more than yesterday – but surely I could take off from the rippling open sea with that. The weather was perfect; a bright sun made the water sparkle and opened up lazy blue distance to the view. Only the summit of Ternate was in a hazy cloud, or was it smoke? Tidore, on the other hand, rose this morning a perfect unblemished cone from the sea. There was a sweet little breeze and I thought a take off would be easy. I ran the 'plane south for a mile-long burst, let the motor cool, taxied back and tried again over the same water for perhaps two miles. The trouble was that at the end of the run the seaplane came under the lee of Tidore, losing both ripple and breeze. There, only the merest breathy puffs wandered vaguely about the surface, scarcely ruffling it.

For once I was not very perturbed by failure – out on that deep blue water with its dancing sparkle, and in the sea-salty air.

I decided to taxi on south between the twins. I felt sorry to deprive the natives lining the shore-front of their fun; but I must seek the breeze through between the islands.

Out of sight from the town both coasts were completely deserted, the narrow base of each mountain a dense jungle of (so it seemed at that distance) pale green scrubby trees, with, on Ternate, an occasional glint from a palm-crest stirring in the breeze. Through the passage, beyond the oily calm I was now in, I could see the dazzling sparkle of blue water. I taxied on slowly, giving the motor a rest. I was lazy, contented and reluctant to leave. The twins, now one on either hand, were fascinating me; each simply a volcano pushed up through the sea-surface, with a mere rim of land round the base. Tidore sleeping while Ternate, its fire smouldering, kept watch. (Yesterday it had been the other way about.) I was glad I had not missed this. Perhaps I was looking at the Isles of the Blest, the fabulously wealthy kingdoms of the Arabian Nights. And I had it all to myself out there .... On one of those perfect days that so often seem to be forerunners of calamity....

I took off at the third attempt, and soon after leaving the volcanoes, left Gilolo on a water-jump of 175 miles to the Talaur Islands. Writing up the log was easy in such weather – while flying higher than usual to escape the hot blast near the surface. 'Interesting to see how far away I can pick up the Talaur Islands to-day. Drift 4° to starb'd 2.23 G.M.T. Wind S.W. by S. Found both my mag switches have stuck – evidently because a screw is loose in same. Flying the highest I have yet – 1,000 feet.' 'The New Zealand Air Force's floats seem in good nick (condition) except for the leaking No. 3 bilge, starb'd. This does not get any worse. The whole 'plane seems to be in as good nick as it ever has been. I took advantage of being unable to get off that day at Ambon to – (the devil! engine cut out for a fraction of a second as I wrote! Those blasted switches, I think) – Ambon to go round with the lionoil pot.' (Lionoil, an oil to prevent sea-water corrosion.) 'Only the prop is getting a bit chewed up. The spray knocks hades out of 'em. Won't last beyond Japan, I sh'd say. Wish I had a metal prop. My dead valve, No. 3 cylinder, seems to be better every day. Can't think why. At Cairns it was quite bad. No compression at all. Monsoon rain-clouds ahead 2.31 G.M.T. Funny how one quickly takes the line of least resistance. They don't like you to say you fly for fun; but I find, if I say I am a writer, it makes them very happy. In the Philippines I shall have to be a company director again, I dare say. But I think I will try author first. I wonder what the Americans will be like to land amongst. . . . My cockpit really looks like a very second-hand shop, books, butter, nautical almanac, mouldy bread, jam-pot, coffee bottle (unfortunately empty), brandy flask (emptying daily), sultanas, string holding throttle lever open, string to make cheese-cutter work, gear for trimming the tail elevators during flight. 02.44, threading line squall. Middle same 02.46½. Very heavy rain east and west down the line. Am going to get through without a drop, I think. 02.49, through line, changed course to 347°. . . . 03.35½ G.M.T. land–o dead ahead. I doubt if one would see it unless looking for it; but still. . . . Rather sleepy. Think I may drop down at the Talaurs for a snooze.' (The Talaurs were forty miles off when first sighted.)

During the half-hour before reaching the islands my obsession to come down in the open sea reached a climax. It had been at work on me for fifteen hundred miles, piquing my curiosity to see whether I could do it and get away afterwards. And now I felt convinced that I could. These tropical seas were so calm. The great danger, of course, was a swell creeping imperceptibly under the surface, which would make it impossible to rise again; but I felt confident that I could detect a swell by now. Feeling guilty, I turned the seaplane round into wind and watched the surface intently while gliding down; everything was right – no drift, therefore dead into wind; no swell; waves short, small and lopping – ideal. The seaplane bumped on the surface and came to rest. But when I tried to stop the engine, the magneto switches refused to budge. I was compelled to turn off the petrol and wait until the carburettor ran dry. There was far more sea than I had thought. *Elijah* rolled heavily, the float in the trough one moment and swept under the crest the next, and I, standing on it, dipped in to over the ankles. It was necessary to keep a firm hold of something. If I went overboard, the rapidly drifting seaplane would have danced out of reach for good before I came to the surface, and Karakelan the nearest island, away to the west, was at a distance where its palm-grown shore was merging into blue haze. Great little seaworthy *Elijah*, rolling to the waves out there under the clear hot sun, with only the slap-splash against the floats breaking into the deadness of sound after flying had ceased! It was right up to expectation, this coming down in the open sea. The strange thing was that

*Elijah* persisted in riding broadside on to the wind instead of weathercocking to it as a seaplane should; I could not understand it.

I lit a cigar; then took the magneto-switch to pieces. The springs were weakened by corrosion with a result that the palls had jammed. I fixed it up as well as I could.

Well, I must leave; I had three hours more flying with another sea-hop of 125 miles.

*Elijah* bumped the waves hard in taking off; every impact shocked the whole machine from end to end. It was an anxious time; but at last she rose. I had misjudged that sea; it was too deep for safety.

As I left the Talaurs behind, I logged this entry, which ought to have been so significant: 'Can see water running from the tail of the starb'd float all the time; so evidently it empties in the air from the same leak' – I thought it came from the bilge, which always pumped a little water every morning.

Sixty miles from Talaurs, as I wrote in the log, the engine suddenly cut out. I was jerked instantly, as a bullet strikes, from tolerant philosopher to primitive animal. As I began the turn into wind, it cut in again and I slowly settled after the shock. I had better climb while I could. When I turned back on the course, it cut out briefly several times. I tried the switches; they were functioning perfectly: it must be due to something in the carburettor. The motor ran smoothly again. After a while in the drowsy, sticky heat I forgot about it.

I made a dead-in-the-eye landfall of Cape St. Augustin in the Philippine Islands; my allowance for drift had been correct. Exuberant with good spirits, I circled the light-house in a steep spiralling glide with engine switched off; and, when nearly down to it, thinking with excitement of coming like this to a foreign country, I absently switched on the motor again. The shock when I realised that nothing had happened in response was like a sudden stab from a red-hot wire. For an instant I was stark primeval man again, only concerned to keep his life, then I had taken in the lie of the water under me, had started all the control movements necessary for avoiding the cliff beside me and for alighting into wind on the sea below, had – finally – looked at the switches, and found them down; they must have dropped again as my finger left them. I secured them with the garter I wore round my knee to hold the log-book and then flew on, relapsing into torpid apathy after the shock.

The sight of a dense black-hearted rainstorm blocking Pujada Bay chilled my spirit and I shrank from entering it; but there was no help. . . .

Through it, a few miles on, I found Mati lying in hot sunshine in baking sultry air.

Time after time I circled the town, as it was called, or village that it appeared to be, but could not see anything of the least resemblance to a buoy or a launch; or even a boat out on the water. There were only some rickety canoes with an outrigger on either side. There was, however, a steamer at the pierhead, and presently I spotted two ship's boats alongside, but could see no trace of a uniform or a flag anywhere.

The water in lee of the pier looked too shallow, so I came down outside and taxied in slowly, expecting to run aground at any moment; but when I cast anchor well inshore of the pierhead I found to my surprise that it was thirty or forty feet deep.

The air was not stagnant, a breeze was blowing; but the heat was like the radiation from the top of a red-hot stove. Within about one minute every nerve in my body was irritated; I felt as if I had a rash all over. There was not a sign of anyone so much as looking my way. Someone on the steamer, by means of a shrill whistle, was directing a cargo winch. I soon found myself waiting in suspense for the next whistle, and each time the noise struck me my nerves felt like hot wires all over my body.

After an age I saw one of the ship's boats approaching; it was a light-chocolate brown, much the same colour as the little brown man standing in the stern and sculling it with a big oar worked to and fro. He could make it go, too. When only ten yards off he was still bearing down at full speed. I shouted at him to stop. He redoubled his efforts. I yelled and swore, almost dancing with rage on the float. It was clear he would ram; and he was coming down-wind against a seaplane fast to a taut anchor rope. I leant far out and caught the stem with both hands. At last, on seeing me strain against his boat, he seemed to recover his senses and used his scull as a paddle to back water. I kept off the bows but the stern swung to one side; then, catching the wind, it came round fast. It would foul the trailing edge of the wing – which was too low to let it pass under – and after ripping through that became entangled in the tail empennage. I waited until it had come round under the wing's leading edge, then suddenly gave it a mighty shove, at the same time thrusting myself back from it and just saving my balance. The boat shot off under the wing with the brown man ducking his head; or else the seaplane shot away from the boat, which had the same effect.

I then went through the long, tiresome business of making him understand by signs that he must let his boat drift down stern first, and hold it against the wind or current as soon as it touched the float. He went away, fetched a mate, and finally landed me at the pier steps. From there I could scarcely make my way up through a jostling, shoving pack of brown folk. Once up, I looked all round, but could not see a single white man. There was an incessant jabber and chatter on all sides; but I could still hear the whistle and the winch on the steamer, and thought, 'That American means to show *he* is not going to be excited by a foreigner.' I felt nonplussed; I could only have made a way through the crowd by force and did not know where I wanted to go. These brown people seemed like Malays with perhaps a little of Japanese in them; but were more perky and talkative than Malays; they were like magpies compared with rooks. I was staring round helplessly when a handsome young blood (brown) elbowed his way through the mob, regardless of anyone's ribs, and addressed me breathlessly without waiting for an answer.

'I am Chief Postmaster. When you leave for Iloilo? Doctor —— of Iloilo wants you to take mail-bag there.'

I thought, 'Damn Doctor ——!' and said:

'Look here, I want to get my petrol before discussing things like mail-bags.'

'Petrol!' he exclaimed as we swayed to and fro, jostled by the surging crowd, 'there is no petrol here.'

No petrol! He could have knocked me over with one finger but for the mob pushing at my back.

'What! No petrol here.'

'No, there is no petrol here.'

A wave of despair flooded me; I knew Mati was cut off from the rest of the island except for bridle-tracks; that communication with the outside world was only by steamer; and here was the steamer now; when would it return? I should be held up for a month; fog would beat me to the Aleutian Islands, and ice to the Yukon.

Yet it was almost incredible.

'Have you no petrol at all?'

'No, no petrol here.'

Confound it! They *must* have petrol. 'But your radio station! How do you work that?'

'Press a key just same as for telegram.'

'But you must have power to drive the generator! Do you use coal, or what?'

Just then a lane was made through the crowd and three more Filipinos strutted up. The Postmaster said quickly, before anyone else could speak:

'I introduce you to Chief of Public Works, to President Elect, and to Chief of Police.'

Good heavens! I thought, I'm moving in high political circles. Well, the higher the better – the Chief of Public Works should be the very man to have some petrol; I asked him, the Chief Postmaster translating. 'No, there is no petrol here.' By now I was as irritated as a wild-cat up a tree; if only I could find a white man. 'Will you take me to the steamer?' I asked. We started but it was almost impossible to force a passage, so finally I asked the Chief of Public Works to send someone on board and inquire whether they had any petrol they could spare me. I watched the man mount the gangway and address an officer – but the officer was brown too, 'Where are the American officers of the ship?' I asked.

'No American officers in ship; all officers Filipino officers.'

Once more I tried:

'Well, in Mati then, I want you to take me to an American in Mati.'

'No American in Mati; all Filipino in Mati; Philippine Island for Filipino.'

No Americans! What on earth was I in for now?

The messenger returned; the officer regretted he had no petrol; but could I not use gasolene instead?

That knocked me right off my haughty perch, I came down to humble earth and started life at a fresh level – their level. I took the Postmaster by the arm and asked him confidingly if he thought he could find me a cup of tea. As we started for the land, up came another Filipino in a handsome uniform, a scout's hat with the brim on one side cocked up against the crown, a tunic with the fine red tabs, of a commander-in-chief, thick riding-breeches generously side-bagged, leather leggings and boots. An egg in one of those leggings laid on the pier would have fried in two minutes, but the officer did not seem to feel the heat at all. He said hurriedly:

'I am Commandant of Military here. The Governor-General has wired to me about you. You will stay at my house. We have expected you two days ago. Where do you come from?'

'New Zealand.'

'New Zealand. Did you stop any place on the way?'

'Yes.'

'No, why that? Do you leave immediately or shall you stay the night?'

I tried to explain things while on the way to the Lieutenant's house. First that my 'plane had only a present range of about 450 miles. They could not understand that. It was an aeroplane and an aeroplane was a machine that made one flight – of whatever distance necessary – and when it landed the flight was over. Did I ever carry passengers? Did I not carry three or four passengers? They could not understand that my 'plane was small. A United States seaplane had landed in the bay and was carrying three or four passengers; and I had a seaplane, there it was in the bay. Did I know that the President-Elect liked flying? It was possible that the President-Elect might be able to find me some gasolene. It was perfectly plain that the Public Works Department, the Police, and the Army all thought they also would like flying. They could not or would not believe that *Elijah* had no room for any passenger, and I sat there – I was now in the Lieutenant's house – having questions and hints shied at me till I felt like an Aunt Sally and did not know which way to turn. And I was beginning to fear they were going to take offence and even turn nasty, when at last the Army said, 'What would happen if Governor-General Davis, Governor-General of the Philippine Islands, wanted a ride in your 'plane?'

'He couldn't have one,' I replied promptly. Then they were satisfied; if I refused the Governor-General it was not necessary for them to feel insulted.

I was now on the veranda of the Lieutenant's roomy house, well above the ground, in the company of all the high officials. Tea, cigars and brandy were served. The brandy, a Spanish or Filipino spirit, was raw stuff, but I drank it gratefully. I tried again for gasolene. They thought perhaps I should be able to obtain some, how much did I need? – a can, five gallons? It was a matter that could be gone into presently, very soon. There seemed to be something mysterious about the gasolene business; I determined to say no more and wait. But I must try for an anchor. If I had demanded the Koh-i-noor diamond, there could not have been much more talk; after a long investigation a weird-looking implement was produced, a wooden crook with another stick lashed across at the other end; it certainly was a kind of one-barbed wooden anchor, but what use would that be if it landed on its back, barb up? And that was the only anchor in Mati, they assured me. I thought I had better use my own though it would not hold in any wind. I went out to the 'plane and, while covering up for the night, the Army and Public Works arrived alongside to be photographed standing on the floats. Then I was taken back to the house. I began to wish I had a musical box which would recite when I pressed a button, 'Yes I am alone. From New Zealand. To England. In the morning. At dawn. For sport.' The Postmaster started afresh about his bag of mail for the Doctor. The Chief of the P.W.D. (Public Works Department) said he wanted to telegraph the exact time I should arrive at Manila to the Secretary of Communications and Commerce. The 'Lootenant' as they called him, then quickly decided that he would like to telegraph the officer of highest rank at my next halt. So I produced my chart. As I had only just taken off with thirty gallons on the open sea at Ternate that morning, I could not rely on getting away with more than twenty-five here, so declared Iloilo out of range; 'That'll fix the Doctor and his bag of mail,' I thought. After a storm of protest and a further long discussion, it was arranged that I should make for Ormoc, Leyte.

The P.W.D. invited me to take a ride in an automobile to see *the* President. I said I would rather have some food and go to bed. But they baited the President with gasolene and hinted, 'no President, no gasolene'. 'Well,' I thought, 'I don't suppose I can become any more tired than I am now'; and we started on a long drawn-out drive in a motor-car, which had only three cylinders that fired, along a narrow washed-out road where every now and then we met and forced aside a bullock and cart driven by a Filipino boy in a large, floppy, straw-plaited hat, and smoking a fat cigar. After a while I began to feel it was all a fairy-story and that I had Puss-in-Boots beside me on the way to visit his master the Marquis of Carabas; for whenever I asked about this or that coconut grove which we happened to pass through, the invariable answer was, 'This belongs to President Lopez'; and whenever we came to a banana plantation, they said, 'This belongs to President Lopez.'

We drove up with terrific horn-blowing to a lofty two-storied house. All its people lined up outside, and then the President took me upstairs to a spacious veranda. He was dressed in expensive-looking clothes, golfing trousers of pepper and salt flannel, black silk stockings, and white kid shoes with brown leather insertions. In the holster that made his cartridge-belt sag at one hip was a perfectly balanced .32 calibre automatic with mother-of-pearl butt. I was allowed to inspect it; but never invited to try it though I threw out nearly as many hints as the Lieutenant had about flying; nor could I persuade the President to try it; apart from this I was delighted with him. He had a giant loud-speaker fastened to the veranda rail, braying out Spanish or some other language unknown to me; it must have been audible a mile away; I suppose the peons, working among the far coconuts, liked to hear it. I was made to listen to it for a while, so that I had a respite from questions, while I enjoyed a cigar of an aroma such as I had never before dreamt of. After nightfall, fireflies, like stars spangling the darkness, jerked and twitched in the black space around. The scent of the tropical night smelled cool in the heat. The President took me off to see his crocodile-house – a roofed-over concrete pool with sides of closely-meshed wire netting a foot high. He shone the torch on a tough, leathery brute, about nine feet in length, lying against the wire on one side. It had an unwinking stare of ageless bestiality, ruthless, cold, merciless; it gave me quite a shock – I recognised a look I had once seen in the eye of a human being.

The President next showed me a large lizard. A cat, busy with its toilet, was sitting on the lizard's back. Then we came to the snake-house and the President shone his torch round the wall. I said, 'Where are the snakes?' He flashed the torch round again; but all I could see was the round beam under the rafters on top of the wall. 'Did I not see it? – the snake had dined only the other day, on a cat, and was sleeping it off. Surely I could see the cat?' Suddenly I realised that the thick bar on top of the wall all round the hut was mottled; and then I saw a bulge like a football in it about ten feet along. . . .

We went back to the veranda and sat for ever. At last, long after I had given up all hope, dinner was declared. I sat next to the President at a circular table which had a round raised centre-piece, loaded with different dishes. This revolved, and whatever you fancied you twirled for and stabbed at, spinning the centre-piece round close in front of all the noses. When we sat down there was absolute silence, except for the clatter of knives and forks and the creak of the revolving table. It was quick work while it lasted; with a few snuffles and grunts we should have been just like a lot of boars round a circular trough. The Public Works was on one side of me and gave me a stern task to keep pace with him; but I managed it, of course. One after another they finished abruptly and we moved away to let the women have an innings. I could not resist a little joke with myself about the

P.W.D. If I were a cannibal, he would have been my beau-ideal.

Every few seconds my eyes would close; I began to drop heavy hints about sleep, hoping for an invitation to spend the night where I was, without having to move again. 'Sleep!' they said, 'Oh, no. No, no. The Postmaster had now the dance prepared and we must return to Mati.' So off we went again, the President before his lined-up household presenting me with three tins of gasolene, some marvellous cigars and a freshly salted wild-cat skin stretched on a wooden hoop; it had been shot by himself the day before, he said. To my surprise the petrol was a gift; I was duly grateful.

On reaching the Lieutenant's house, we found the vast central room cleared of furniture. Some remaining spark of vitality in me was fanned up by the prospect of a lively evening among the maids of Mati. After all, a dance had great possibilities. I changed into my suit, prepared to dazzle the local eye. A band duly arrived; later, coy maidens, done up tightly in dresses of stiff brocade or similar stuff which looked Spanish, drifted in from the darkness, each guarded by a chaperon – for the most part wizened crones with monkey-like features and a vulturine eye. I was led round and introduced to them all, one by one, with a long speech every time, of which I did not understand a word; I could only try to smile intelligently, and not feel silly. . . . I can just remember that I danced once or twice, that I thought them stiff, keeping their distance, and wearing modesty like an armour, where they needed none at all; while the hags watched step by step.

My drowsiness became more and more hard to withstand, and at last I waylaid the Lieutenant, thanked him firmly for his great kindness, but regretted that, as I was falling asleep where I stood, I must beg to be allowed to retire. The poor fellow was much put out and thought me a dreadful boor, I'm certain. I only remember that I was shown a bunk; that, as I fell on it, I estimated the big drum was beating four feet from my ear through the thin partition; and that I was asleep in two seconds.

## CHAPTER XII

### AN UNFORGETTABLE MEAL

IN the morning I suddenly remembered my promise to send a message to van Brink of Ternate and with guilty haste consulted the Postmaster. He was anything but enthusiastic. As far as I could make out, the message would have to be relayed through Manila, Borneo and Batavia; after he had talked about it for a while it seemed a fantastic enterprise; finally, although Ternate was only four or five hundred miles away, he quoted a frightful price of about two dollars a word. I thought, 'that may just leave me with insufficient money to reach Manila'. I weakly gave in and denied my promise to send it. So I failed to keep my promise and saved the money; but found later that my conscience had been debited with the item.

A Spaniard turned up and, through the erratic interpretation of the Postmaster, offered me two tins of gasolene. My heart warmed with all the more gratitude for the generosity of a man who could not even talk to me. He was largely built, round-bodied and full in the face, with an exceedingly white skin and small deep black moustache; he seemed quiet and passive, like a cod stranded among a lot of flighty goldfish.

The Postmaster kept at me until I consented to carry

a few letters to Manila in a sealed mail-bag. After that, the President and the Treasurer, each with his revolver in his belt, had themselves rowed to the seaplane and photographed standing on the floats. The President signed himself President Salvador P. Lopez, but his official seal in my Journey Log-book read Municipal President, Municipal Government of Mati, Province of Davao, Mindanao.

My next delay was due to the anchor fouling the coral bottom. I heaved and tugged every way. (I now had a length of wire cable next to the anchor, having found that the coral cut through rope like a knife.) Finally an obliging Filipino dived down in about twenty feet of water and freed it for me. Everything seemed ready at last, and I was just about to start the engine when a banka came rushing out; the man paddling it, in a state of great excitement at thought of missing me, made straight for the floats, and never slackened his pace as I naturally expected. When only a few yards off I suddenly realised this and let out a roar. He immediately dug down his paddle hard and backed water. This depressed the stern beneath the surface; the rickety banka filled and slowly sank. The Filipino kept his seat and tried to wield his paddle in the rising water; but the banka went on sinking until only his head remained above water. Then he stood on the banka, pathetically crestfallen at the shout of laughter and derision from the pier. But the banka settled deeper and deeper till only, the man's hat and the top of his head showed above the water. At last he must have been floated off, for he began struggling in the water, while the banka slowly rose again to the surface and supported him. By the time I had my camera out he had begun to appreciate being in the limelight, and within a few seconds was flashing his white teeth at me in a brilliant smile. The letter which the President had decided at the last moment to send was rather wet.

In spite of the sultry heat there was a fair breeze blowing and I took off at the first attempt after a long run. Twenty-five minutes later I came upon the steamer, which had left the night before. It was lying in a bay and, in a fit of enthusiasm, I dived down at it; but not a soul showed on board – they were at lunch, I suppose – whereupon I begrudged the loss of height and the return to the grilling heat at sea level.

The country was undoubtedly beautiful, but I was not interested. I had seen enough of it to last me a year and enough Filipinos to last me ten years. All I wanted was peace and quietness, comfort and easy flying that required no effort from a drowsy brain. To lunch as well as possible was all I cared about. I investigated the parcels of food given me by the Lieutenant. A chicken leg in one was quickly disposed of; a plain loaf of bread in the other was helped down by some of the Cairns butter; and this, I recorded in my log, should be very digestible judging by the ease with which my nautical almanac had absorbed it. After lunch I had brandy, coffee and a cigar; it was my own brandy and good, the coffee was excellent and the cigar superb. But, though I kept my head well down, smoking in an open cockpit did not yield a tenth of the flavour of the night before. This, curiously enough I thought, I attributed to my ears; either to the noise or the wind in them, or to their being covered with the helmet.

Soon after lunch I had to pass through a rain-squall twenty-five miles wide. I realised grudgingly that it might have been worse; but skimming the surface in torrents of rain was a fatigue, and while sitting tight the constant working of the rudder with either foot gave me cramp in the buttocks. Later on, I struck another rain-squall which gave me a thorough fright. It was close to the point of land shortly after passing Ilongos. The great drops of teeming rain had at once beaten the surface dead flat and covered it with thin spray. It was like flying through a dull grey cloud; I could not see the water at all, yet knew I was only a foot or two above it. I had to make an instant decision; but it was all so sudden and unexpected that it caught me drowsy, and instead of alighting on the spot while I knew the water was close underneath though I could not see it, I shied, banked and began turning. Immediately I had done so, I cursed my unutterable folly. I had no blind-flying instruments, and with nothing but a compass could only fly in cloud provided I made the gentlest of turns; by turning steeply I had at once locked the compass needle with centrifugal force. So that I was now in the same fix as a man flying blind in a cloud without any instruments at all; that is to say it was almost impossible to tell how the 'plane was flying – which side uppermost even – until out of the cloud. But here instead of cloud all round I had the sea somewhere close to one wing tip. Sitting tense, all drowsiness blown away by the shock, I summoned all the skill I knew and all the touch I possessed to keep the 'plane level in the turn. In a moment, the low beach loomed up under the wing tip, and I was following it, swearing that never again, so long as I lived, would I be such a fool.

It must have been the calm centre of a tiny cyclone that I had struck, for on emerging I found the wind from the south whereas it had been from the north on entering. The air was now cooler. The speed-indicator tube had been put out of action by the rain.

In the middle of the forty-mile Ormoc bight lightning flashed close beside me, and sent my heart to my feet. The wind began changing direction rapidly, the sky was overcast a dull grey, night seemed to be falling, and I was full of dread and depression. Also, having allowed only a twenty-minute margin of fuel supply, I was anxious lest some unforeseen incident should delay me. But this did not last long; my spirits soon recovered. I did not seem to care so deeply about things nowadays. I lit a cigar and drank some brandy; and in due course arrived safely at Ormoc.

I did not take the trouble to circle the place; but came straight down under the lee of the pier and cast anchor. While the bankas drew near, I stowed away my gear, piled my haversack and bundle of clothes on the wing and covered up ready for night so as to save myself the fag of boarding the 'plane again.

Before I finished, the natives were therc, and I was shouting almost continuously, while making signs to one after another for them not to squeeze the leading edge, wrench at the ailerons or clutch the tail elevators. They seemed a strange mixture of cockiness and timidity. As soon as I was ready for shore I beckoned imperiously to one and climbed into his banka, treating it all as a matter of course, and without taking the least notice of him. This worked excellently; there was no jabber and he paddled me straight ashore. When we beached I was faced by a mob of natives, uttering loud cries, who made it impossible to move a step. Somewhat at a loss, I clutched my bundles. Then I had an inspiration. 'Take me to the President,' I demanded, 'the President, the President, THE PRESIDENT.' This quietened them a little, there was an impulse to make a lane for me, and I was just going to force my way through when a little man in trousers which were whiter than those around me and long instead of short, arrived and buzzed like a human mosquito. At first I was annoyed; because my President plan seemed to be working so well without any palaver. He could partly understand my meaning, but only with a great deal of hard work in stating each sentence many different ways. He said he could speak English well, but *mine was so bad*; he was Provincial Attorney and the only man in the town who could speak English. He wasn't a bad little fellow, when you became used to the unceasing hum and constant attempts to settle on your attention. I should have been more grateful to him than I was. When we reached the President's house, the young Attorney marched straight up the outside stairs; and about two dozen of the mob at our heels – as many as could win footing – pushed their way up too, until the unfortunate President's house rather resembled a bamboo crate full of jabbering brown natives. At first I felt sorry for him, for having me and such a rabble foisted on him without so much as a by-your-leave; but I stifled my conscience by thinking he deserved it for not keeping his presidency in better order. Later again I was sorry; he turned out to be a fine fellow. He was short and stumpy, with a squarish head securely set between his shoulders; his face was a dirty brown colour, lined and seamed. I thought at first that he simply did not know how to deal with the mob, for he stood there slightly smiling the whole time and nodding his head; but later I decided this rather inane smile was only a kind of mask behind which his brain worked shrewdly enough. He rarely spoke, keeping silent till he had thought out exactly what he wished to say. His house ran like clockwork, another sign that he was not such a foolish old man as his smile made him look. I judged him by his hands to be a manual labourer. He could not write – someone guided his hand to sign my log-book. The Attorney said to me, 'Our President is working-man like your own (Ramsay) MacDonald.'

I had made up my mind to put the onus of finding a lodging on to him, but he seemed to take it as a matter of course that I should stay in his house. And what a meal he provided! First soup with chicken-legs and other pieces in it; and a plateful of rice to each person (there were eight at the table – all of the one family, I think). This rice was eaten in tune with the soup. I had been caught before in relying on another course which failed to arrive, so I dined well off this one. But there followed an oval dish as big as a tray, piled high with chopped meats, onions, potatoes, and all sorts of oddments, and ringed by boiled eggs half-way round the dish, and tiny lemons round the other half, while another dish of rice was placed alongside each of us. The rice was as delicious as the meat, and I rather gluttonously finished a helping as large in itself as a substantial breakfast. But no sooner was this course at an end than a large fish came steaming in; each rice-plate was removed, and another, piled high, took its place. Politeness forbade me to give in; but worse was to follow; my third plate of rice was removed, a fourth took its place, and in came a monstrous lobster-patty. By the time that had been disposed of, I was struggling feebly, though resolved to die game. A following dish of apricots nearly gave me the opportunity. Even the President was forced to take a few turns about the room.

I slept on a bed of tightly-stretched rattan like the open canework used for chair seats. Even I needed no covering in that close and moist heat, and slept well as soon as the rustle and furtive whispering behind the thin partitions had ceased to tease my imagination.

I awoke at dawn and looked through the shutters – there was no glass in any of the windows – at the water. The house was alongside a creek where it joined the sea and both were oily smooth. A small two-masted fishing-boat lying in the creek had a narrow thatched roof suspended above the deck from end to end like an awning. To my Occidental eye this had a Chinese look; decidedly, I thought, I was travelling north. There were a few palms near and a creaky bamboo footbridge, occasionally crossed by natives in dirty white singlets.

. . . . . . . . . .

Ten o'clock. I had been out in Ormoc Bay for nearly an hour. The surface was glassy-smooth; the shore fringe gleamed dully in it. At first I had tried north-west into the head of the bight, treacherous water sown with rows of upright fishing-stakes, often only projecting an inch or two, and it made my flesh creep to think how they might just as easily be an inch or two below the surface as above it. Also there were isolated stakes difficult to see in the blind spot ahead of the plane when driving across the bay with motor roaring at full blast, propeller beating, the heavy lifeless air with double noise, nose of the seaplane cocked up, and floats shearing through the water like huge twin ploughs. I drew back from the shore-line and charged it again. I was in a petulant rage; this was ruining the motor and the propeller, and bad for the whole machine. A launch approached; I sank my head in the cockpit – Lord! How I was sick to death of damned natives and trying to make myself understood. Last night trying to buy an anchor – trailing through the streets from store to store, with a screeching mob of boys behind me. What an aristocratic community Mati seemed now compared with the rabble of Ormoc! The launch had gone; it must have been on its way somewhere or afraid I might need a tow. I never took any notice of the natives now; if I regarded each one as having individuality it was too exhausting. I ignored them or lumped them all together as 'natives'. . . . I must try again to take off; it was no use, but there were seven U.S. Army 'planes due to meet me outside Manila. Well, I should not be there to be met. I was sorry, but it was not really my fault.

Perhaps it was the prospect of a reception that made me more than usually irritable to-day. . . .

An hour and twenty minutes later. Well, here I was still, after trying twice more without success. I was a fool to lose my temper before. After all, it was delightfully peaceful on this water; the stillness, with the motor shut off, was indescribable. Air, water and land seemed half dead; but the heat was everywhere. Occasionally, very occasionally, the surface would pucker with faint arrowheads from a light puff of air, the arrowheads having two barbs on either side if the puff were stronger than a mile an hour. Lord! wouldn't it be lovely here in a boat. . . .

One o'clock, still on the water. I had made seven attempts and emptied three gallons of petrol. Curiously enough, the 'plane was every time as near as could be to taking off, but jibbed just at the final lift. I sat on the wing while the motor cooled off. After one of the attempts I had tried all the bilges but found them 'pretty good'. Well, from now on I would keep trying in the same direction round the headland instead of returning over the same water each time. . . . At least I should be taxi-ing towards Manila. . . .

Two o'clock, five hours at it. Well, I liked this game. I could beat the 'plane at it, too, in the end – provided the engine held together.

2.20. I investigated a suspicious noise; and traced it to one of the magnetos. I hoped it was all right; but even if the damned engine ground that one to bits, it was still going to take me into the air on the other. Two spark plugs in the starboard set had given out. And the motor was rather short of oil to-day.

After each failure I opened the petrol-cock and let the reeking spirit patter on the taut wing-surface, or, changing its flow, dribble down the centre-section strut; then patter again, until another two or three gallons had been jettisoned. I would certainly get into the air in the end, I might have only enough petrol left to fly back to Ormoc, but, by heavens! that 'plane should fly. . . . Already it had taken me fifteen miles across the bay from Ormoc. . . .

'2.55. Left water in heavy rain. Had emptied petrol to 17½ gallons (3½ hours' fuel). What place is there on the chart about two hours' flight away? Palanog seems the only one. Palanog, nog, noggin, what a gorgeous sound! It might be a good place. Nogging of rum! A cask is what I want. Palanog, 4.40.'

## CHAPTER XIII

### GOVERNOR CORDOVA – AND AN EARTHQUAKE

IF inclined to condole with myself over Ormoc Bay yesterday, it was a mistake; I should have saved up my feelings for Palanog, or Masbate, which they indignantly assured me was its correct name.

This time I started off with only eighteen gallons; and there was a seven-mile breeze to help. It blew from the head of the inlet, so that I ended up my runs where steepish hills narrowed the bay to a point, and countless jagged fishing stakes stuck out of the water. The township was nearly out of sight, though not more than five miles distant. At each attempt the motor vibrated more. The propeller-tip had now a piece out of the edge as though bitten through by slanting teeth. It must have struck a piece of floating wood or coconut in the first place; and flogging the spray gradually widened the gap and unbalanced the propeller more. All the while the tropical heat seemed to suck up my energy, draw it from every limb. Squatting on a float in the shade of a wing I took my notebook and wrote: 'It would break your heart, this game; I have been out here since 9.30 and it is now one o'clock, or is it two o'clock, I have forgotten.' I had kept on trying time after time in a straight line for the head of the bay. I had noticed in a dull fashion that the seaplane was taxi-ing starboard wing slightly down. Then, when I opened up the motor, the starboard float buried itself in the water, like a submarine submerging. For some distance I could not rise it above the surface. I simply could not account for this; ponderously I laboured my brain to discover the cause. I was dull-witted; six hours in Ormoc Bay, followed by the earthquakes all through the night. . . .

. . . . . . . . . . .

Last night. . . . On arrival at the Governor's house I had noticed several large poles in the main living-room of the upper story; these poles rose through the floor in the middle of the big room and were evidently part of the structure. To one of them a piano was securely bound with coils of stout rope. It had looked odd. But all through the night I was woken up by earthquakes. I counted up to eleven of them. They seemed to seize the house and shake it violently until it rattled, and every article in it chattered. The shakes were uncanny and weird, like nothing on earth; the world seemed to be dissolving underfoot; for an instant one's doom seemed to be at hand and one's soul poised indecisive for flight. The inhabitants' attitude was certainly strange. . . .

. . . . . . . . . . .

I brought my wandering thoughts back to the distant end of Masbate Bay and to my seaplane stuck there. My first belief had been that the float had struck one of the water-logged coconuts drifting about almost submerged. So I tried all the bilges again; but they only pumped the usual quart or so. The only possible explanation now was that the starboard wings had become water-logged, and looking up I found the little drain-holes along the trailing edge had never been punched through the fabric. I opened one near by with my knife and some water ran out. My heart leapt – the mystery was solved! In my rubber shoes, carefully balancing, I walked along the rear wing-spar pricking the holes open. But no more water ran out, so I decided it must be the bottom wing at fault. The trailing edge of this I could not reach without a boat. Bankas rested on the water here and there, drifting round the shore-edge like wildfowl; there was one just across from the seaplane. I hulloed and waved my handkerchief; they paddled the other way like men possessed. The more I hulloed, the further and the faster they paddled away. I stood on the cockpit and waved a handkerchief on the end of my walking-stick. I kept at it, waving and hulloing for about twenty minutes. Suddenly, on turning round, I found another banka had come up behind, with a little fellow in it and his family watching me, open-mouthed, passive, curious, like animals watching the first man they have ever seen. The man was dressed in ordinary European shirt, hat and trousers. He might have been a brown yokel from any country; but his children – if they were all his – looked some like young Japs, some like Malay boys. I beckoned, he drew near. I climbed in and manœuvred the craft under the lower wing so that I could see if that were water-logged. But no more than a cupful of water came from it.

I tried again to take off. . . .

Well, the float-bottoms must be foul; that was the only possible explanation remaining. I must get back to the town. The wind had changed to north. Perhaps I would try once more near the town. Manila seemed as close and as far off as freedom to a man in prison.

But when I came to taxi now, I could not keep the plane on a straight course; when I speeded it up, it promptly went round in a circle. I kicked on full opposite rudder and pushed the throttle open to the limit, so that the big tail surface had a blast on it which should have made it jump round; but the only result was that the starboard float drove in under water and went on submerging until the wing too dipped in. I switched off before the 'plane capsized. I tried streaming my drogue behind the port float; but it had no appreciable effect, the seaplane still went round in circles. I climbed out along the wing and streamed the drogue from the outside strut – where it had about as much effect as a bucket behind a liner. I was stuck, and well stuck; I could not even get back to the town. The seaplane would probably founder where it was. If I did get back to the town I should be stuck there, for months, until a new propeller arrived from Sydney. And that would mean the end of the flight. . . . What did I care? . . . The heat seemed to press on one's brain. . . .

. . . . . . . . . . .

This morning it had been terrible. The church bell began ringing at five o'clock, three strokes at a time. Whether that had anything to do with the earthquakes I could not tell. Then the interminable discussions in nursery English: 'I want ten gallons of gasolene. Can I buy gasolene? Where can I buy gasolene?' repeated time after time, word by word, until I had nearly sent myself to sleep. I had not eaten any breakfast; my head ached and I felt as if a fever were coming on. I packed and stood about waiting while the Governor sent boys round the town to find other boys to carry my gear down to the wharf; when that had been done he decided that we ourselves should go by motor. More boys (or perhaps the same boys) had been sent to run the town for the motor. Each time a boy returned there had been a long discussion and then the boy was sent off again. Finally a car arrived; but, instead of going to the wharf, it went to the government offices, where I was introduced to Treasurers, Attorneys, and every kind of official. They appeared to be all working in a big room like schoolboys, each with his desk, and dressed in clean whites. Ways and means of obtaining gasolene were discussed with every official. Finally the town presented me with twelve gallons and we left on a hunt for oil; we seemed to visit every shop. I was inclined to think the Governor chose the hopeless ones first; in them he was the man of authority bending with affability to his people; he would state my need at great length and with the tolerant good-nature of a man not personally concerned with the issue. In the end I had bought some of the most suitable oil I could find. Then began a search for something to put it in. The Chinese Filipino storekeeper was astonished at my taking notice of the dirt deposit on the funnel and in the bottom of the tin. When I remained obdurate, he produced his handkerchief and wiped all the vessels clean with that. Down on the wharf there had been a discussion about a banka. Governor Cordova still wore his genial air of affability; but now I began to wonder if under it he were not actually tongue-lashing the more earthy of his people. The native who finally brought up a banka had been, I thought, very self-conscious. His craft was the craziest imaginable, a narrow canoe made from a hollowed tree-stem, high perched and with no outriggers. Being in it, was like balancing on a tight-rope and every second a peril of the deep. Fifty natives on the wharf shouted directions and encouragement. We went round the 'plane in three circles before I could make the man understand how to board it. And then, with the canoe end-on, I had to step from the quivering high-pointed stem on to the toe of a gently dancing float. I stowed my map, and haversack, package of clothes, camera, watch and the rest; checked the tappet clearances; emptied in the oil and prepared to leave. A native arrived with a letter for his third cousin in Manila. Then the anchor had refused to come away; it had fouled in the coral. . . . All the business of getting a diver to free it. . . .

. . . . . . . . . .

I pulled myself back to the present; my mind was almost wandering; I was in a kind of daze. Well, the only course left now was to send a message for help. I had never been forced to do that before. . . . I signalled to a banka hovering undecidedly in the middle distance; it was different from the others I had seen, had a cocked-up prow curving gracefully, and a drawn-out stern sweeping back over the water to a point. I scribbled a note:

'To the Governor,
'Masbate.

'Will try once more to leave the water. If I fail will you send a BOAT to TOW ME in to Masbate? There is something WRONG with my engine. Thank you.'

I looked up to see a motor-boat approaching, a top-hampered, palpitating, unbalanced-looking craft; the Governor had sent his secretary to find out what was wrong. The motor-boat circled in front of the 'plane and I asked for a tow. I threw out a line, but they missed it four times, the man at the wheel going full-speed ahead each time he drew near the rope; when at last they picked it up they attached it to their *bow*, and proceeded *across* the front of the seaplane at full speed. Now a side-pull on the float of a seaplane will hardly turn it even when it is riding light – but will only make it glide forwards or backwards. As soon as the rope fast to the bows of the motor-boat took the strain, the motor-boat was swung round like a toy in a pond, and made straight for the seaplane's tail. I shouted at them to cast off the rope, but either they were taken by surprise or else they still expected the seaplane to come round; for they held on and I waited for them to crash into the tail empennage. Then someone on board collected his wits and cast off the rope. The motor-boat missed the 'plane.

Now they picked up the rope at the first attempt, secured it to the stern, went full-speed ahead, and stalled the motor-boat. By this time we had drifted to within fifty yards of the shore, and I rigged my anchor; but the motor-boat started once more, picked up the tow, and brought the 'plane safely across the bay. I disembarked at once; I could not be off the 'plane soon enough. I felt I wanted to curl up somewhere and turn off existence. . . .

We walked up to the Governor's house. The heat was terrible; it gave way only with reluctance to our passage. We found the Governor doing nothing; when in that state he seemed to suspend his being and if interrupted he must first recall it to animation: one could follow the return of consciousness by watching his features.

My feverishness had gone (whether owing to the strong dose of quinine I took at the third earthquake I could not say) and I was hungry. Cordova was most considerate and promptly ordered a meal for me, shouting to the womenfolk, who seemed to lead a shadowy existence in some gloomy part of the house out of their lord's sight. I went and had a bath in the room with the floor-joists left open for water to fall through to the ground under the house fifteen or twenty feet below. They never used the ground-floor of their houses. Above the noise of water splashing I could hear the chicken being killed and very soon it arrived, cooked and in pieces. Chewing it would have delayed even a fox for some time; nevertheless, I enjoyed it and, feeling better afterwards, accepted Cordova's proposal to look for somewhere to beach the 'plane.

Cordova's personality was more developed than that

of any Filipino I had yet seen. He looked experienced, as if he had a past, and was now leading the life of a model citizen. He had charm, and could flatter you that you were worth far more than you yourself imagined – and this with an air of complete indifference which was very effective, and must have gained him a good many victims of either sex. He had a dark face and black glossy hair with a strong hint of Spanish blood in him.

We motored round the harbour till we found a stretch of mud shore that I had to admit was suitable. It was filthy and sprinkled with small, snail-like sea-shells and little pieces of scoria. On either side were native dwellings roofed with palm-thatch and built high off the mud on sticks; at full tide the mud under them was covered over with water. We drove back through a wild profusion of palms and broad-leafed juicy plants, mostly banana and tobacco. On reaching the wharf I suddenly thought I would open a manhole in the float before beaching the 'plane. The sea was smooth enough not to swamp it. The manholes, as I called them, were round openings in the top of the float, one or two to each bilge compartment, and just large enough to admit a man's arm. I opened up the front one without dropping a single screw in the water. The bilge was perfectly dry. I said, 'I open one more?' Cordova replied, 'Go ahead,' so I set to work on the back manhole of the large middle bilge. When I removed the cover and saw what was inside I just stayed where I was, on one knee, cover in hand, eyes fixed, staring, until Cordova called out, 'What is it?'

This middle compartment, about six feet long, was half full of water; there must have been forty gallons in it, equal to nearly half the weight of the whole seaplane. The pipe running down to the bottom of it had been struck by the keel when the float-bottom had had a knock. This had cracked it, so that when I fixed my pump to the top it sucked air through the crack. In a kind of stupor I pumped till dark and lowered the level considerably; then, leaving off for the night, I went down the street muttering, 'God bless my soul,' and 'Well, I'm damned,' till Cordova began to look sideways at me. To think of my disgust, and rages, and despair – at Brisbane, where swerving the seaplane had lifted that float out; Whitsunday Passage, where it had made the seaplane swerve and nearly capsized it; Rockhampton, Merauke, Amboina, Ternate, Ormoc. To think of my pumping that bilge and always finding it dry! The hours I had spent on the water, the gallons of petrol jettisoned!

And now that I had discovered it, it was too late – the propeller was ruined; why it had not broken up altogether that morning was a marvel. I was stuck in Masbate for at least two months – it was too horrible.

Then later as I lay on the bed I began to think. Could I possibly reach Manila with the propeller? It would not be so bad waiting there. 'I wonder if I could mend that propeller somehow.'

'How could I possibly do that?'

'Other things are mended; why not a propeller?'

'Even if it could be mended, I know nothing about propellers.'

'Well, find out.'

'I might bind the tip to prevent it breaking up more. But what with, cord, insulation tape, wire?' I had been told that an aeroplane propeller, unbalanced or with the airfoil of one blade changed, would vibrate the motor till it broke clean out of the fuselage.

Then I had my great inspiration – try a kerosene tin! And with that I went to sleep so soundly that I must have nourished all the unemployed mosquitoes of Masbate; the net was too small to cover both head and feet, so I knew I must risk one or the other outside, and thinking the buzz would not disturb my feet, they were the ones to be left out wrapped in a sheet. However, the mosquitoes must have bitten through, for in the morning the flesh felt solid with bites. I was woken again by the church bell at five o'clock; which made me think it must be the custom and nothing to do with earthquakes; because there had been none during the night that I knew of – except for a tremor or two before I went to sleep and scarcely worth mentioning.

The attitude of the inhabitants towards the earthquakes had been peculiar; everyone we met the day before had chattered to Cordova about them. From those who were airing their English for my benefit (or their own gratification) I gathered that everyone *said* how terribly serious they were, that a big eruption might overwhelm the island at any minute, *and had the Governor telegraphed to the Government at Manila about it?*

I pumped the bilge dry – that was simple enough – and then set about removing the propeller. In order to reach it, I had to stand on the tip of one float, lean over till I lost my balance, and with one hand on the propeller boss, keep myself from falling, while with the other I unscrewed the bolts. Each bolt was held by a lock-washer, and there were about a dozen bolts. I soon lost one spanner, and though the native dived for it he could not find it. I tied another to my wrist, at the same time tying a handkerchief round my brows to keep the sweat out of my eyes. There was no breeze and with the sun striking up from the water as well, it was like working before an open furnace in winter clothes. Underneath me in the light milky-green water gaudy tropical fish flitted about. There were some perky little fellows in black and white vertical stripes, and a large number of pallid white squid, all head and tentacles, like long mushroom tops with arms trailing from all round the edge. They moved along in a steady succession of jerks by puffing water out behind, and I half expected to hear a chug, chug, chug as they drifted by.

As soon as I had the propeller on shore I cut a piece out of a petrol tin and worked it into a sheath for the tip. I gave the Governor five cents to buy some shoe tacks with. He returned with drawing-pins, which I considered hardly the thing for an aeroplane propeller; so I sent him off again; this time he brought tacks, and I completed the job, binding insulation tape round the other blade, partly because it had been damaged a little partly to balance the tin, and partly out of curiosity to see what would happen.

The difficulty of replacing the propeller was even greater, but at last I had it trued up with one blade exactly tracking the other. I covered up the manhole of the bilge, which was making about a gallon every three hours, and swung the propeller. The engine started, and the propeller seemed all right. I taxied faster; the 'plane responded easily to the controls; I was delighted and opened up the throttle. *Elijah* rose into the air like a bird. Suddenly there was a terrific din. Flap! flap! flap! I thought a blade was broken, switched off instantly and alighted on the spot. But it was only the tape coming unwound and whipping the float at each revolution. What I could not understand was how the tape threshing round at 400 or 500 miles an hour should be quite undamaged. I took it off altogether. As soon as I opened up, the 'plane vibrated violently like a shaking-machine at a country fair. The front cockpit palpitated in front of me and I could scarcely grasp the throttle. I thought the engine would be wrenched from its bed and flung out, and though I must have closed the throttle instantly, it seemed an age before the engine stopped.

This time I took the propeller to Cordova's house, sheathed the other tip, threaded the propeller on my walking-stick between two chairs, drove in tacks till it nearly remained horizontal, moved another tack along the edge until the propeller balanced perfectly, drove that tack in, and the job was done.

This time the seaplane flew admirably, and Cordova had been such a willing helper that I offered him a flight. I packed him in the front cockpit among the gear. The 'plane would not rise from the harbour with his extra weight, so I taxied out to the open sea. There I found a fair breeze and just the right sea running. We were bowling along merrily, engine at full blast, Cordova bubbling with glee – there was no windshield to his cockpit, so that the 100-miles-an-hour slipstream driving right into his face produced a sensation of terrific speed – when I felt a jar; the port float had struck. Looking straight down I found, to my dismay, that we were in the middle of a coral reef. I switched off at once and alternately eyed the float, to see if it were going down, and the reef behind us. As soon as the seaplane lost way it began drifting backwards before the breeze. Most of the coral was alive, many-branched shrubs of it in varying hues of red. Suddenly I noticed a broad clump, with seaweed streaming on the surface, straight in our line of drift. I jumped out of the cockpit, landed on the float, slid into the water up to my waist, and held on waiting until I touched. At first the seaplane's way ran me off my feet; I could feel the coral harsh and jagged through my rubber soles. Then I secured a good footing, stopped the 'plane, and fended her off sideways; feeling for a foothold under water at each step, sometimes finding no bottom and falling in a little before I could pull myself back to the float; but every now and then getting in a good push at a pace that seemed like a run under water, until I passed the seaplane round the side of the clump, jumped for the float, and landed with my body across it. Next moment my feet touched again, and so I jumped from clump to clump, with wild scrambles back on to the float, until I had guided the seaplane back into the channel. From down in the water I could see Cordova still bubbling with glee, wrapped up in his own experience, intoxicated by the thrill of speed. He seemed to think it was all part of the game for me, in a pair of tennis shoes, to be pushing him round a coral reef in a seaplane. 'Damned amusing,' I thought, 'if I missed my footing, my boy, and you found yourself drifting across the Samar Sea all by yourself.'

When we were through, I told him about the float striking and that I must get the 'plane back as soon as possible. He was perfectly satisfied, wanting no more thrill than that of taxi-ing at forty miles an hour. No doubt, as the only man on the island who had been in an aeroplane he would be the flying oracle for years.

To my surprise and delight, the port float was intact; which showed how sensitive to any unusual happening a pilot becomes; for it must have been only a scratch for the thin duralumin shell not to be ripped open by coral.

Next day, in the air: – 'Left Masbate 3.45 (11.45 local time). Took three photos. 4.15 *Steel Traveller* (Steamer). Am just sitting in the sun enjoying myself. Cigar and coffee. Steamer, 4.45; didn't read name. . . .'

## CHAPTER XIV

### WELCOME AT MANILA

THREE United States Army 'planes met me fifty miles south of Manila and flew above me in formation. I felt embarrassed every time I thought what a silly little aeroplane they must think mine, or how difficult it must be to make their 'planes fly slow enough, and what a nuisance I must be to them. Alternately I was excited; I had reached Manila and it was thrilling every time I looked up in the hot sunlight to see those fighters keeping steady formation above my head and the pilots sometimes waving to me. Such an experience would not happen to a man often in his lifetime.

When I had come down at Kavite outside Manila, they swooped like three roaring hawks; then zoomed to their flying field.

Later, after my vessel had been granted free pratique by the U.S. Quarantine officer on condition that rat-guards at least three feet in diameter were worn on all lines leading from vessel to shore, I was driven in to the Manila Hotel, and Bagtas, the Secretary of Communications and Commerce and President of the Governor-General's Aviation Committee, led me straight to a man sitting in a large wicker chair, close by the tall entrance archway.

'I'm Williamson,' this gentleman said. I murmured something politely. 'Where's that letter you have for me?' he asked.

'Letter!'

'The letter you have for me in your bag.'

I searched in my baggage, and he was quite right, I had a letter of introduction to him from an acquaintance of mine in Sydney; but not intending to present it except in extraordinary circumstances, I had forgotten all about it. The letter had been in my knapsack in Cordova's house, and as far as I knew, had never left it. I remembered that Palma the Provincial Auditor at Masbate had been made correspondent of the Manila papers, a young gusher of unctuous goodwill and perky questions – the sort of questions one instinctively desires to parry. I had seen a lot of Palma and heard more, a veritable human sandfly out for his victim's news; however, he had rewarded me with a signed photograph of himself in a mortarboard and gown, with 'from the man who insisted getting facts from you' written below the gown and 'Provincial Auditor' rubber-stamped above the mortarboard.

As I sat drinking a whisky and soda and Williamson mopped his brow, he invited me to stay with him. He was the Manila manager of a cold storage company, which went in for shipowning as a sideline to icemaking. I thought he ought to make a fine business man: in the first place, he was born in Aberdeen, and in the second it would be impossible to move him from his stand when he saw that he could hold it; and if forced he would quietly compromise. He had a steady air of weighing every event carefully. And he proved to me that no one in the world is more hospitable, quietly and unobtrusively, than the Scot, when once he gets started. We drove out to his house, a well-built, well-planned, two-storied place, and my host proudly pointed out that in a typhoon, no matter what quarter it was blowing from, one side could always be left unshuttered. He had designed it himself, even to the details, and superintended the building of it for his firm (this was the Manila custom for firms to own their managers' houses); it was lined with Philippine mahogany and other timbers, which were beautifully grained. The garden and surroundings were delightful; partly Old Country style with orderly trees, wide, well-mown lawns, shrubs and flower-beds, creepers and ramblers. But it was apt to make me forget I was only fourteen degrees north of the line, and in consequence, I think, I wrongly struggled with the effects of tropical conditions.

After a bath and a change, Williamson took me in to the Manila Club – the English club – to join a cocktail-party. I had never been in such a British atmosphere before. I was made to feel very much at home and extraordinarily welcome; presently I began to wonder why, after due allowance for the influence of gin slings, I was talking so much more than usual. Then I realised that I had slipped back twelve years and was at an English public school again. Most of the men were cable, or army and navy turned oil. The bloods were apparently taking to oil instead of the diplomatic service nowadays. Soon I was pleading for mercy, for ginger-beer instead of gin, and after taking me to meet the newspaper reporters at the hotel, Williamson drove me home to dinner. He was a modern Aladdin; only, instead of rubbing a lamp to obtain anything I liked to suggest for dinner, he spun the key of an ice vault, and so we had some excellent grouse. It was a good dinner and, after it, he took me to the monthly dance at the club, where I was introduced to so many people that I began to feel like a little boy in curls and a sailor-suit pushed into the drawing-room for exhibition at a tea-party. The heat while dancing was terrific; even the whisky and sodas could not cool me; I felt that partners should be dressed with zip-fasteners down the back so that they could go off for a cold shower after each dance. At midnight, after a few final drinks, I was whisked off to the Manila Hotel for another dance; 'which,' they told me, 'would be brighter.' I began to think I must have flown upon a lost tribe of two-bottle men, and invoked the shades of my ancestors for prowess; however, Williamson assured me it was a special occasion. By 3.30 when we reached home, it was hard to believe that Cordova and his coral reef belonged to the same age, not to mention the same twenty-four hours. Now, on returning late, Williamson used to enter his house through the 'boys' ' quarters at the back. Neither of us had any matches and it was only after some trouble with the latch-key that we discovered the door had been left open for us. A few steps in the passage-way, and there sounded the noise of a toe stubbing something metallic, then a stumble and a loud thump. 'Sh!' I said, 'you'll wake your madame.' I heard a noise like the mutter of a Scotch volcano preparatory to eruption. 'Why! it's an anchor or something. Who the devil piled all your seaplane stuff in the passage?' There was now silence except for the rustle and respiration as he made his way to the light-switch across the kitchen. Suddenly there was a hair-raising cry, 'Great Scott!'

'What's up?'

'A damned animal jumped at my face.'

'Keep still,' I suggested, but next instant the glaring light went on. I tried hard not to laugh, but the sight was too much for me; for what should be dangling from a line across the kitchen but the President of Mati's wild-cat skin. 'Gr-r-r, man, what d'ye want wi' th' dom' thing anyway? I could ha' shot a dom' sight better in me own backyard last Thurrrsday morrrning!'

A strange thing about people in Manila was their attitude towards typhoons. Everywhere I went I heard the same question, 'When *is* the typhoon coming?' But it was not in order to pack up and leave that they wished to know; they were complaining of the lack of one[1]; the sultry heat was every day growing more oppressive; a typhoon would clear the air. Typhoons hardly ever struck Manila itself, but were directed north or south by a mountain range, apparently never climbing a range if they could go round it.

Work was started early in the city, and at 7.30 Williamson lit his cigar, and his Filipino boy chauffeur drove us in through a park of gorgeous flower-beds.

[1] They had not long to complain. On the 14th. following three-quarters of Manila city was under water, and bankas paddling up the main streets were the only transport to the offices.

In the city proper it was difficult to move, every street was so densely packed with natives that it resembled a muddy, living canal of brown faces and dirty white clothes, in endless commotion and occasionally parted by a motor-car.

My first call was on the British Consul-General, Thomas Harrington, Esq., who by his presence made me think of Great Britain as a Power – and not a shop for which he was advance agent. First he let me know he disapproved of not being notified about me by the New Zealand Government; obviously he had never been to insular, independent, happy-go-lucky New Zealand. After that he proceeded to do everything he could to help me, and took me to the Japanese Consul-General, who put on a wonderful smile and darted about with quick, excited movements like a hen which has only managed to hatch one chick and mislaid it.

'Yes, his country allowed me to make an aviation to Japan on the following conditions and aerial routes:

' "Aviation is prohibited in the air of the following districts: –

' "Over or near (1) the S.W. coast of Formosa; (2) the S.E. coast of Formosa; (3) the Pescadores Islands on the west coast of Formosa; (4) the north coast of Formosa. . . ." '

I might come down at Tamsui in Formosa, but my route to it was laid down exactly; I must not approach the coast for the first eighty miles, but fly out to sea; must then approach the coast, and fly over the town of Karenko; then cross the island south of a line drawn through Giran, Tooyen and Tamsui. This meant crossing a range of which five peaks were known to be over 12,000 feet; it was doubtful whether my seaplane could climb to half that height, so that I should only be able to cross by finding passes and threading a way through the mountains.

After Fosmosa I was forbidden to fly anywhere near the Ryukyu Archipelago connecting Formosa with Japan; this would force me to fly to China in order to reach Japan.

As for Japan itself, I was only to touch at three places, and for the rest of the flight must keep fifty miles out to sea. I was furious; it was not so much their forcing me out to sea, forcing me to fly to China, or forcing me to cross the China Sea, that enraged me as their forcing me over the mountains of Formosa.

I was not allowed within fifty miles of Tokyo; I should have liked to take the goodwill letter they had asked me to bring to their Prime Minister in Tokyo from the New Zealand Prime Minister and publicly tear it into little pieces in the middle of Tokyo Bay.

Afterwards I told Harrington about some of the difficulties the Japanese were making; that the Ryukyu Islands formed an almost continuous chain from Formosa to Japan, that with one stop half-way I could do the flight; that going round by way of China meant, besides all the extra negotiations necessary before flying to another country, a 500-mile seaflight.

He said, 'Well, I'll go and see him again for you; but you'll find it difficult to shift them once they get anything into their heads. And, of course, this fellow is under the thumb of his superiors at Tokyo, and has no say of his own. However, I'll ask him if you can get permission to land somewhere else in Formosa and at one of the Ryukyu Islands.'

He then took me to the Manila Hotel, where the Governor-General's Aviation Committee was giving a lunch for me. I was put next to Bagtas. The Filipino on my other side, so Bagtas informed me in a loud whisper, held an office equivalent to that of our (meaning Great Britain's) Minister of the Interior. The party was entertained by a man at the other end who read out the bluest stories I had ever heard, from typed sheets in his hand, until I could see even Harrington's diplomatic geniality wearing thin; for this I felt drawn to him as a fellow-sufferer, and because he was a sportsman. Now I had been told to invite anyone I liked: so had asked several, including two U.S. Air Corps men, Major Duty and Lieutenant Valentine, both splendid fellows. My embarrassment was therefore acute when I saw that everyone except Harrington and myself had to sign chits and pay for their lunch. I dodged making a speech by proposing the health of the President of the United States, and a second time by proposing that of the Philippine Islands. The function closed with a toast to H.M. the King of England, drunk in cold water.

Afterwards I had a talk with Duty and Valentine. Duty said, 'You flew right through the prohibited area, straight over the forts.' I said, 'Good heavens, did I really? I'm frightfully sorry.' To which he replied, 'Oh, that's all right,' and added that the Air Corps would do anything they could to help me.

The Manila people were out to give me a good time. I was taken to the Polo Club and swimming-bath, where I grew depressed, watching the women and girls bathing; out to dinner; to a boxing-match (where I was astonished at the punishment taken by the little brown lightweights and at their skill). But every fresh show of favour only made me more depressed, more lonely, made me feel more like a specimen at the other end of the microscope. To them I was an idea, a quality responsible for the success of bringing a small seaplane from New Zealand to Manila. I began searching each face for signs of particular, not general, friendliness. I wanted intimacy, intimacy such as that between two persons who had thoughts and feelings in common, who mutually shared experience and mutually supported each other. I looked round, and it seemed a state of bliss to be settled in a roomy, rambling, old house-shell surrounded by beautiful orderly gardens, like these young men with their charming young attractive wives, while the day, the night, was their common property. Sometimes I day-dreamed of a Devonshire meadow thick with buttercups near a stream, sometimes of being alone on a yacht, lying on deck doing nothing but lazily sail it across the Pacific. Then grew the longing to stop being respectable, stop behaving properly; I wanted to run wild, I wanted licence, vice. But the more fiercely this desire, instinct, raged, the more bitter and strong was the grip of caste or heredity or cold-footed respectability that prevented me. If I misbehaved it would shame the faces of these extremely British men; and my feeble hints for wild parties in private they affected to misunderstand or turned by saying, 'Just wait till you get to Japan, that's the place,' or 'You should see So-and-so about it, he's the man.' 'Well, where is he?' 'Oh, he's away for a fortnight.' Then I became absurdly sensitive; the more I liked any woman, the more stilted became my conversation with her, and I would avoid her for fear people should talk about our being together. In any case, I told myself, it would be useless to see much of her, since in a day or two I must be gone. I became profoundly depressed, existence was utterly futile, I lost every ordinary appetite for food, wine, song, play, work, everything that I could have for the asking. I became irritable and touchy with only one taste remaining which I could indulge – for jokes, chiefly petty ones. Williamson and Mrs. Williamson were patient and forbearing, and never complained; only he warned me one night, after I had been pulling a reporter's leg over the telephone, that I ought to be careful lest the papers turn nasty. But the reporters drove him, too, to exasperation. I think they believed that to be like the smart U.S. reporters they must get news by trickery; and being Filipinoes it was an unimportant detail if there should be no news to get. Williamson declared that he did no work from the time I arrived. One evening we were sitting on his veranda when he unexpectedly said, 'Hullo, and who the deuce are you?' and I turned to see a white face – so it looked in the dark – with large eyes staring at us through a pair of enormous horn-rimmed spectacles. A young fellow stepped up to the veranda and said he was 'student at the world-famous Manila University, also friend to the great Artman Igneo Middletoza. They were both enthusiastic aviation; his friend the Artman had made portrait of Mr. C., and would he be so good enough to sign him?' 'Let's see,' said Williamson, and the youth handed up a piece of cardboard with a scribbling on it like part of a cogwheel's outline. Williamson said he thought it a remarkable likeness, and then began ragging the boy, whom I set down for a youth with an attack of aviation craze. I felt a little sorry for him; for the virus of that disease can be as bad as unrequited love, and make one as silly; so I answered his more sensible questions, such as 'Would I please tell him when I leave so that he and his friend could see the machine which flew such great space act?' But when he asked 'Wasn't there great danger?' I slipped a trifle from the narrow way, and next morning the paper had an account of an interview with me in which 'I had revealed the great danger of flying – ptomaine poisoning from the tinned food carried'.

There was a philatelist there, Bruggmann, by name, who was persistent in his endeavours to make me carry more air-mail. A shrewd business man, his Swiss-American-Jewish volubility was difficult to combat.

One night he was sitting in a wicker chair on the veranda talking as usual while the moths flew round us, and a whisky and soda stood on the table before him. Suddenly there was a plop. I saw something on his arm; a house-lizard had fallen from the ceiling during a skirmish. Then I saw another lizard in Bruggmann's whisky and soda; it was resting with its forepaws on the rim of the glass, and its long head, a shade browner than the whisky, pointed almost vertically upwards, staring at Bruggmann's face as though hypnotised. Bruggmann did not stop talking

– he had not noticed. His hand closed on the glass; I held my breath, fascinated by the prospect of their meeting face to face; but Williamson said, 'There's a lizard in your whisky.' Bruggmann went on talking. 'There's a lizard in your whisky and soda, Senor Bruggmann.' 'Ach, yes,' said Bruggmann and, scarcely interrupting his flow of words, flicked it out with his little finger as if he were always flicking lizards out of his drink; then gulped down the whisky.

Williamson's 'boy' drove me to the seaplane at seven o'clock. The company owning the Philippine Islands' private seaplane had lent me space in their shed, and my machine had been wheeled in from the sea on an axle. The floats were in a bad way; I could see daylight through the keel of the starboard; the other had a bad bump, and long scars showing through inside where Cordova's coral reef had nearly entered. I felt depressed; not only did a float repair require highly-skilled work on thin sheets and rivets of duralumin, a most refractory alloy; but also wealth to pay for it. A new float cost £250, and the work of making a new one was probably easier than that of repairing an old one, since the latter must be done by touch alone, the workman's arm filling the manhole. My three or four pounds still left, and the forty-six pounds more which I expected, would not take me far if required for float repairs as well as for the petrol, oil and expenses of the voyage. However, the first thing to do was to take the floats off the seaplane. This appeared simple enough; but at the end of a whole morning they were still on. And my chance of getting them off without smashing the aeroplane looked small.

The company had two pilots and the one on duty that morning was a bony-faced German with a sloping forehead and thin hair brushed back from it; when he talked he used abrupt sentences of quick, run-together words. Now the obvious way to remove the floats was by first slinging the 'plane to a principal of the roof; but the German issued from his den and would have none of it. Well, if the roof principal gave way under the strain, besides my 'plane being smashed, a timber joist belonging to the company would be smashed too, and as he was the company's servant, I could not proceed against his orders. I suggested something else which would only damage the floor if the seaplane fell during the operation; but he would have none of this. Then I suggested a scheme which would have involved the seaplane only, if it went wrong (and I thought it was very likely to); but he pooh-poohed it so abruptly and decisively that to carry it out would have been equivalent to telling him he was a liar. He appeared to be extremely irritable; I began to fear he could not be fond of me. I felt a wish to say, 'After all, it *is* my machine and my risk'; but it seemed impolite and, besides, I could see his point of view – undoubtedly I, an amateur, was the spoilt pet of Manila, while there were veterans of the air far more deserving. I went to talk with him in his office, and was astounded at his flying experience; he told me he had flown nearly every type of machine. What! Was he flying in the War? Hch! in the War! he flew all through the War By Jove! what squadron was he with? One of the American squadrons, not the Lafayette, by any chance? Hch! he wasn't fighting for *us*. Oh, really!

I was most interested and full of wonder at his experiences, and presently tried to induce him to tell me how my seaplane ought to be lifted – a cook can often get the same old joint eaten by serving it in a different way. What he did not know about aeroplanes was not worth knowing. Now, what did he think would be the best way to lift the seaplane? Oh, there were many ways in which he could do it. I think the best was to tilt the 'plane up on one wing tip. I meekly suggested that perhaps the insignificant and rather frail 'Moth' was probably not one of the important types that he was used to handling. Hch! he snorted, he had handled dozens of them in China.

It was a depressed, baffled, abashed and despairing amateur pilot that Williamson's Filipino fetched for lunch. But after lunch the other pilot, an American born, was on duty, and we had the seaplane suspended from the roof in about thirty minutes; the floats and propeller off by tea-time.

The floats were in a bad way; when, on the New Zealand Air Force Moth, they had been dragged up the beach at Samoa every night, the heads of the keel-rivets had been worn off, thus allowing the sea-water to act on the dural; then a length of stainless steel had been laid over as a false keel, and the corrosion had continued behind it. The stuff we had taken for putty, when painting the floats at Lord Howe Island, had really been the residue after chemical decomposition. Roly Wilson's paint alone had kept the water out in places; fortunately it was fine paint and handsomely laid on; the dural crumpled in my fingers.

My only hope was the U.S. Air Corps. Was their

offer of assistance merely a conventional politeness? I rang up Nichol's Field; it was not, and Major Duty in charge of the Ordnance came round at once. He inspected the floats, said they were in a bad way, and that they would repair them for me; also the propeller. Next morning at 7 a.m. an Army lorry arrived and took them away. Duty was a short, round-faced, round-headed man who talked in a low-pitched monotone; was extremcly pleasant, interesting on material subjects, and as efficient as the devil; if told to level off the 7,000 Philippine Islands he would have gone straight ahead with the necessary organisation, and started on the following Monday with the northernmost island – or perhaps one in the middle of the group so that he could level all ways at once.

I set to work on the engine; wearing overalls only – I found them cooler than shorts – and a handkerchief round my brows. No wonder the citizens complained; the heat was like a hot substance in the air.

Clear, an English engineer, lent me a Filipino mechanic to grind the valves – a job I detested with its eternal twisting. This Filipino did not talk. It was true he had no English; but even to other Filipinos he rarely talked while working – to the policeman, for instance, who was set to guard the 'plane, and who dozed out the day in his chair in the sun. The exhaust valve in No. 3 was so pitted that we threw it out. The magneto impulse-starter, which had been noisy at Ormoc, now seemed in good order; it must have been seized by the heat, which had been intense enough to melt solder on the cowling above.

Duty invited me to come and see the floats and look

round Nichol's Field. I thought this would interest Clear, so I rang up to ask if I might bring him. 'Who do you want?' demanded the orderly at the other end of the telephone. 'I want to speak to Major Duty.' 'Major Duty? There's no Major Duty here.' 'Why, dammit, man, I was talking to him myself only five minutes ago.' 'Wait a minute, I'll ask.' After a delay the voice said, 'Do you mean Major *Dooty*?' 'Yes,' I said thankfully, 'I do.'

They made a splendid job of the propeller, splicing in a piece of wood, and then sheathing thc tips in copper. This made it heavier; but it was now obvious that only metal would stand up to the constant slashing through spray and wave-crests. The propeller was on a spindle and so well balanced that when I breathed on one tip it began to revolve. I congratulated them; Cordova and I could not have made a better job.

The floats would take some days yet. On their turning a hose into one, the water had gone straight through. The riveter declared he must cut a hatch in the top in order to drive home the last rivets. We all stood round offering suggestions of how to avoid this; and at last it was agreed that he should screw the last plate to a block inside instead of riveting it. Who could foresee the consequences of such a petty detail? By the time the floats were finished, 600 new rivets had been used, each one driven by hand.

The officers wives not yet having left for Harbin in Manchuria, where they go at the hottest time of year to cool off, or so I was told, I was invited to several all-American parties. The American women made pointed remarks about my beard; but I noticed they had at the same time a great curiosity about it, and, whether they doubted its reality I do not know, but they often seemed to have an itch to feel it. One extraordinarily attractive girl came waving a safety-razor round me one evening, and I was forced to put her in the bath; afterwards I could have kicked myself for handling her like a china statuette instead of a woman. Their figures were magnificent and showed to the best advantage in their after-dinner pyjama suits; they took free and easy strides not only physically, but mentally, too; talking like men, only with quicker, keener intelligence, while never forgetting to look seductively feminine at the same time.

It would soon be a half-year since I left Wellington, New Zealand (including the time spent on the way learning sextant navigation and seaplane flying at Auckland, and in rebuilding the 'plane in the Tasman). 'Five and a half months of solitary existence on a ship would be less lonely than this flying game,' I wrote. 'On the ship one would at least become used to the craft and all the parts of it, the sails, the ropes, the cabin, the decks; but with flying, one is no sooner acquainted with any place or person than one must leave them and fly on again.'

These were only land thoughts, of course; life in the 'plane, in the air, was a life apart, strange, secret, thrilling, to be put out of mind when down to earth, not to be thought of in the midst of sullying materialism. I was now a third of the way to England, had 12,865 miles yet to fly, by way of Aparri, Karenko, Naha, Kagoshima, Shingu, Nata, Nemuro, Broughton Bay, Petropavlovsk, Attu, Atka, Dutch Harbour,

Nulato, Fort Yukon, McPherson, Fort Norman, Fort Providence, Fond du Lac, Port Churchill, Cape Wolstenholme, Chidley, Frerickshaab, Angmagsalik, Reykjavik, Thorshavn, Aberdeen, London.

Having asked the Manila branch of the Oil Company to make certain that my petrol had been sent to Broughton Bay where the three Japanese scientists lived, Chichagoff and Nazan Bay; and now hearing that a reply had arrived from Japan, I went in to see the manager. After waiting for some time on alternate feet in a roomful of Filipino clerks, I was admitted to the presence of the great man, an Australian I think, who was spraying orders round like the merchant prince of a penny novelette. (I had prickly heat and, in addition, a violent cold which seemed an injustice in the tropics; my skin had dried up and I was peppery-tempered.) The Japanese branch had cabled to say they had no instructions to lay down petrol in the Kurils. I was furious; only one or two steamers ran there annually and Sydney's failure to order the petrol might prevent me from crossing that season.

'But that was the last thing I arranged with your company; they were to cable immediately for the stuff to be laid down, and I was to pay for it in Japan.'

'That's all very well,' he said, 'but you have no credentials from our firm in Sydney; all I received was a telegram from Hong-Kong, "Chichester arriving using our products".'

'Well, I've stuck exclusively to your oil since I left Sydney, paying full price for it and risking my motor through being unable to obtain it often enough, in order that your Company could have any advertisement that might eventuate; so now it's up to you to find out why supplies have not been laid down for me.'

After some warm words he cabled to Sydney and when he read out their reply, 'Chichester must make his own arrangements,' there was thunder in the office air. 'Well, what are you going to do about it?' I demanded. 'I will cable to find out the cost of laying down the supplies, but you must first pay for the cables.' I thought, 'So, if I buy the butter I must first pay for the cow.' Well, they had told me to make my own arrangements; I would. I stamped out of the office, across the street, and up to the Shell Company opposite, who arranged for petrol to be laid down at two islands in the Kurils and two in the Aleutians.

On Sunday I was bidden by Mrs. McCoy to dinner. Her husband had commanded an American regiment at the capture of Manila in the Spanish-American war of 1898. My uncle had commanded the British ships sent to Manila to watch our interests, while the Americans, the Spanish and the Filipinoes were fighting. Trouble was brewing between the Americans and the Germans who had sent a squadron under von Diedrich and who were at that time looking round for chances of colonial expansion; but Chichester stood by Dewey and, when Dewey moved in to bombard, moved his ship between the American and German fleets; which was considered a pretty broad hint to the Germans.

I had a great admiration for my uncle; so that his having been to Manila and taking part in such an episode had made me wish to fly there.

The other guests at McCoy's dinner were from

Government House – or whatever the Governor-General's official residence is called in the Philippines. I was a very small one amongst many, all strongly allied by Government House atmosphere, but I resolved on a brave front behind my borrowed white dinner-jacket. However, it was not till the marrow-bones that I felt the ground at all sure under my feet. I had last tasted marrow-bones twenty years before, at my great-aunt's, who though over ninety had yet wit enough to keep the best cook in Devonshire; and she had had wonderful old silver marrow-spoons, long, narrow-fluted scoops; somehow I felt better for it now.

The Governor-General was a big man, slow of speech; he seemed to be a man with an easy power; anything he did would be well within that power and never overstretch it; and he was cast in such a big physical mould, that he must have a generous, easy-going nature.

The dinner was excellent; the only thing that puzzled me was the liqueur brandy served with the soup. Filipino independence seemed to be the great local topic. When I had arrived at Mati and heard all the talk of 'Philippines for the Filipinoes', I had thought it a joke; but now I gathered it was not, and that the Philippines in a less serious and more comic form were America's Oriental Ireland.

After dinner we sat under trees overlooking the bay with its still black surface and its few lights showing long-drawn yellow reflections. A genuine gecko called 'geck-o-, geck-o, geck-o' from the depths of some shrub.

Harrington thought the Japs had long ago made up

their minds about my request to have the route changed, but that they delayed saying so in order to impress me with their importance. However, word came through at last – they refused to let me call at any island in the Ryukyu Archipelago. And with mighty seals their Consul-General sealed up my camera which took photographs the size of a postage-stamp. An American told me it was all a bluff about the Ryukyus, that they had nothing there to conceal – and I thought he ought to know judging by a map of Japan which he showed me; it was marked with submarine bases, naval bases, navy air stations, audiphones, disposition of 'planes, troops, guns and stores, and a lot more. I could not help laughing – was it possible that foreign powers knew all the secret military dispositions of this people, who became so fanatical if they thought a foreigner wanted to approach within ten miles of a military zone!

I was now fretting to leave: Father Miguel Selga, Director of the Weather Bureau and a charming man, had a typhoon up his sleeve. Every day he used to visit me, when I was working at the seaplane, and tell me with a kind of satisfaction how a depression was slowly forming east of the Philippines, how it had formed, and then how it was intensifying. Finally, on July 30, he called it a typhoon, and on the 31st handed me a typewritten notice, 'Typhoon warning. The Pacific depression or typhoon was situated at 10 a.m. to-day to the east of northern Luzon in about Long. 126° E., Lat. 17° N., moving probably north-west.' And I think it can be said that on this day began my strange race with a typhoon which a few days later was to destroy 2,000 homes in the Ryukyu Islands near Formosa, and which the *Asahi Mainichi* was to describe as the worst typhoon of the century. A typhoon was, of course, far more dangerous for a moored seaplane than for a ship. A gusty wind of only fifty miles an hour could overturn the seaplane. A seventy-mile wind would blow it out of the water. And not only was it astonishingly difficult to find anywhere to house a seaplane on land, but it was almost impossible to handle one to get it ashore in a high wind. But I was not greatly worried at that time. A typhoon was only likely to travel at one hundred miles a day when young, and no more than three hundred when older, so I thought I could easily turn round and flee from it if I could not carry on and fly from it. My only concern was to reach the north end of Formosa before it. Formosa was my only possible outlet northwards from the Philippines, and it was almost certain, judging by the track of previous typhoons which had started from the same spot, that this one would make for Formosa.

Meanwhile the typhoon was 150 miles nearer Formosa than I was. Next day, July 31st, it had not begun to move; nor had I. On August 1st the floats and propeller arrived, the paint on the floats still wet. I put on the propeller. Now I had a little depression of my own; there was something demoralising, humiliating, about taking help without giving anything in return for it; all these people helping me solely in order to further *my* achievement made me feel utterly selfish, which in turn made me angry. Then everything went wrong, spanners slipped, nuts cross-threaded; people continually interrupted me. When the propeller was on I found, to increase my rage, that there was no compression whatever in any cylinder. All the while prickly heat was irritating me, my cold was abominable to me, my decapitated finger throbbed continually; it was the climax when the motor absolutely refused to start; I could not get one kick out of it though I swung the propeller till I couldn't see for sweat in my eyes. I could have seized a sledge-hammer and smashed the whole machine. Suddenly I perceived myself a stupid little microbe making fantastic infinitesimal struggles, of no account whatever in a universe. I laughed, returned to the house and went to sleep for a few minutes; awoke a different being, went back to the 'plane, and found it child's play to take the electrical connections to pieces, clean them in petrol and replace them. The engine started immediately; after two minutes running the compression was perfect; the whole aeroplane and the floats were in admirable condition. I had not a care; even Father Selga could not worry me with his old typhoon which he said had scarcely moved but could be expected to start at any moment.

The seaplane was launched with complete success, the sun shone, the sea sparkled and danced. The motor had a harsh full-throated bark that was music in my ears; *Elijah* rose as lightly as a snipe, skimmed to and fro over the surface trying out her paces (the greatest speed a modest ninety-six miles an hour), zoomed and dived, frisked and chased her tail in tight circles, inspected the Polo Club's flagstaff, fanned the trees, and looked in upon Nicol Williamson (who was laid up with dengue fever).

Brimming over with enthusiasm I returned and offered a flight to Clear, who had helped me launch the 'plane. 'It's worth a month's existence,' I said.

'No, I don't think so, thanks.'

I was astonished and tried to coax him; but he resisted all my blandishments; and so did four more of my helpers. It is really remarkable how many people, when I offer them a flight have been asked by their wives not to fly, or who have asked themselves not to for their wives' sake.

After lunch (a good fortifying lunch, I think) Millett who had lent me my white coat for the dinner-party, changed his mind; so I turned out the gear stowed in the front cockpit, and installed him in its place. Even with him aboard I had 100lb. less weight than I should need on the morrow to reach Aparri; the seaplane refused to take off. In silence I tried this way and that. After several abortive attempts, Millett turned round and said, 'Ha, ha! Have you warmed up sufficiently to take off yet?' At last I wrenched her off, and after a short flight returned in gloom. Next morning there was no breeze at all and I had the greater load, so that my spirits sank during the exchange of ceremonious farewells with the officials and friends come to see me fly away. An anticlimax in a theatre was bad; in real life it was dreadful. From seven o'clock till ten I refused even to try. Then the glassy calm was faintly stirred by a gentle breeze, boomerang ripples appeared, and I made the first attempt.

Presently MacIlroy the American pilot came out, took off ahead of me in his big seaplane, and made bow-waves like a ferry-steamer, but they were of no avail. After that he remained near for a while; but I told him I might be out in the bay until three o'clock before being able to take off.

My spirit was utterly weary; had I not *yet* done with this interminable ploughing of dead still water? this flogging of sultry air? How long must I endure it? How many hours of it had I been through?

Plap! I looked round in surprise. All I could see was a piece of wood rocking in the surface; it settled to rest, lying flush. I turned away. Click! There it was again; a piece about two feet long and twenty paces away from the seaplane. Nothing else was visible, and the air scarcely breathed on the surface. I waited with eyes fixed. A minute later a lean, grey back, dorsal fin erect, cut through the surface, butted the block of wood in the air till it slipped off sideways, then silently submerged again. Pop! Up went the wood again; and time after time it was butted up, now from one side, now from the other.

How I longed to be fishing, with nothing else to do or think about!

The sea gradually calmed me to resignation – I might be worse off than I was. I took my kapok jacket – intended to kep a pilot afloat for three days – made a pillow of it on the wing, and went to sleep with one leg hooked over a flying-wire. I awoke with a jump that seemed to lift my whole body. With a deafening roar an army 'plane had dived on me. I stirred myself, sheepish at having been caught napping; I found a ten-mile breeze now blowing.

I tried twice more, then pumped forward some of

my petrol. The plane seemed to go better so I opened the cock and ran off petrol till the back tank was empty. That left me with twenty-seven gallons and the motor burned five gallons an hour, so that I had five hours twenty minutes fuel supply. The flight was 403 miles, so that at seventy-five miles an hour I had a five-hour twenty minutes flight. However, there would probably be some place where I could come down if I ran out of petrol. It was terribly hot on the aluminium-painted machine; I could hardly keep my eyes open; the moisture-laden air was like a drug.

When I was up (for the seaplane now rose at the first attempt), I had to fly back to Williamson's house to let him know I was off at last. He waved to me from between two of his typhoon shutters. It cost me nearly twenty miles; but I was glad I had done it.

It was now a case of trying to keep awake, and sufficiently clear-witted to calculate distances and petrol consumption. I took no interest in the coast-line; it seemed dull country. (My mind was growing tired, and I was beginning to close it to unessential sights and feelings.) I had no appetite for writing, and only made a few notes on the map:

'1 hour, 68 miles.

'1½ hours; favouring wind; now making 93 miles an hour. Doubtful if petrol will get me to Aparri. 19 gallons left.

'2 hours; made 90 miles last hour.

'2½ hours; estimate 3 hours petrol left (15 gallons). Might make it if wind keeps good.

'3 hours. 83 miles last hour. Wind veering to W. by N.

'3½ hours. Speed 78 m.p.h. 128 miles to go; not quite two hours petrol left. Can do it. Tin of tuna interrupted by storm. S.S. *Mauran.* Heavy rain-squall. Wind, lightning. Driven out to sea for 20 miles, back to coast at Cape Bojeador. Saturated. Chilled to the bone. 4 hours 9 minutes out. Finish tuna.'

When I alighted on the Aparri River, after circling the town for some time, it was exactly five hours twenty minutes since I left the water at Manila; but I still had some petrol left, I rocked the 'plane on the water and could hear it swish in the tank; there must have been a gallon or two there yet, so that I could have been spared much of my anxiety.

## CHAPTER XV

### OLD MALVERNIAN

APARRI proved full of surprises for me. It was built on flat, low mud ground beside an islanded river. This appeared lifeless from the air so I flew over to rouse the town. I dived down at it and circled it, but no one in the street took any interest. A few merely glanced up. This was strange; in all the world I would have said there was no place more likely to display fanatical enthusiasm on arrival of an aeroplane than this isolated little township at the end of the Philippines.[1] I came down on the water, and there I might have stayed had not an American casually passing on his way home after work given me a lift ashore in his launch. He was the manager of a timber-mill, Frank W. Sapp, grizzled and cynical, a crisp hard nut in a tough shell; a man, I should say, who had continually to deal with numbers of hard-living men. He kept me outside his shell and parried any questions I asked. There was something attractive about him, but it was soon apparent that I could get as much information out of an iron bar. However, he ordered a native back to the seaplane to guard it, and then took

[1] American Army seaplanes had been based at Aparri while photographing unexplored Luzon from the air.

me to an hotel. That was my second surprise – a dirty old two-storied wooden pub. On the ground it had a many-doored bar with chairs grouped round a number of small tables. My eye immediately caught that of a young man at one of the tables. There was something familiar about him. He had a fresh complexion, looked – perhaps by comparison – as if but recently out of a bath, and his nose was even brighter than my own, a fleshy pink which would have surprised Turner. Then I realised what was familiar – I knew his tailor. Sapp had gone, or at any rate I was not conscious of him.

'Hullo!'

'Oh, hullo.'

'I'm Chichester.'

'I'm Smith.'

'Devilish thirsty weather.'

'Devilish.'

'Does the bowl flow here?'

'Rather! Boy! two bottles beer.'

'Never expected to find you here.'

'Oh, I often come up.'

'Look here, were you at Marlborough?'

'No, Malvern. Why?'

'I don't know. I thought I knew you.'

'Were you at Marlborough?'

'Yes.'

'Were you? I thought you were Moulin Rouge or something.'

He told me the hotel was owned by the old woman sitting behind the bar, an extraordinary character, a Spaniard, people said; but no one knew; and rumour had it she was ninety. He pointed me out a man at another table who was said to be her lover; a fierce-looking brigand with huge moustachios, with one eye that looked piercingly at you while the other rolled in its orbit; who was evidently in a quarrelsome mood, waving a tankard in the air, banging it on the table top, periodically breaking out into song.

'Everybody stays here,' said Smith, 'Pinedo was here eight years ago.'

'Good Lord! Am I still following that chap's trail? Tell me, what the deuce brings you up here?'

'Oh, I sell milk.'

Instinctively I looked around and outside the door.

'Tinned milk, of course.'

Presently a Filipino came to thc table; he appeared rather sour. He said the officials and citizens of a certain town (I could not remember the name) wished to know when I was arriving there; they had been telegraphing all over Luzon to find out what had happened to me.

I asked what town it was and he named a place of a quarter million inhabitants (I think he said), the capital of some province, and sixty miles inland.

'But I could never fly there.'

The officials and the people were very indignant to hear I had flown to Aparri.

'But my aeroplane was a seaplane, it was not able to land at this place.'

The Secrctary of Communications and Commerce, Senor Bagtas, had said I should land there; he had wired to say 'Expect him at three o'clock this afternoon.'

'But I had a seaplane and could only –'

All the officials and all the people had been waiting for me for four hours.

'But a seaplane –'

They had cleared the parade-ground for my machine.

'But a seaplane –'

More than dissatisfied, he left me.

Time passed rapidly until, in the middle of our talk, I suddenly remembered the 'plane and its guard. We stumbled down several wrong byways in the dark before we came to the water's edge. With some difficulty Smith persuaded a native boatman to venture forth. We crossed a number of barge-like craft littered with sleeping natives who grunted and chattered and grumbled when we trod on them; sometimes we passed through a hut built on board – these huts arched the deck from side to side, and were made of nipa-palm thatch on a hooped frame. Then we set off down the back-water in pitch darkness on a huge cumbersome bamboo craft poled along by four men. We barged into every boat moored the length of the backwater, and streams of voluble chatter would pour from the craft we lumbered into as well as from our own.

Now we were out in the river and began searching for the seaplane by shouting for the guard. He was still there crouching patiently on a wing-root. The anxiety I should have been suffering for four hours instead of talking to Smith now flooded me all at once, and I had a guilty conscience about my neglected duty. However, flashing the torch round, I could see no sign of the native having put a foot through the wing. Only most of the new paint was off the floats where he had been standing. We took him off. The boatmen were amazingly skilful; handling logs in a forest makes a man skilful in handling any vehicle, and I wondered if in the same way the handling of logs in water (for big logs, presumably mahogany, were lying all round, spiked and tied side by side), made a man skilful with boats.

That night lying under the dirty mosquito-net of the hotel bed, I wrote up my log, scarcely able to see the paper by the dim yellow light penetrating the net, and intermittently trying to catch the mosquitoes inside it; the Aparri mosquitoes seemed to have a particularly fine physique.

In the morning I inquired for news of the typhoon; but no one seemed to have heard of a typhoon coming, nor did anyone take the faintest interest in it, and, as the day was perfect, bright and sunny, I assumed it had only been an eddy in Father Selga's meteorological imagination or had simply evaporated.[1]

With Smith I made my way out to the anchored 'plane. When I stepped from the boat, the float I landed on went straight under water. The wing dipped in, and still the float went down; the seaplane was rolling over. Recovering my balance as quickly as possible I scrambled across the boom. With my weight on the other float, the seaplane slowly righted. Then Smith and the man in the boat held down the wing tip on the buoyant side while I gingerly recrossed the boom, and began pumping. The leak was

[1] Aparri is in the usual typhoon pathway and is struck by more typhoons than any other town in the world.

in the same old bilge. I pumped for about ten minutes, but feared the water was gaining. I therefore instructed the boat to tow the seaplane close to the shore, so that it would be in shallow water if it sank. The shore was a low bank of silt and sand with a coating of slime an inch or more thick. Slithering about on this and standing up to my waist in water, I removed the manhole. The float-compartment was about two-thirds full. I baled it out with the large tin that could be passed through the manhole – a tobacco tin. When only a few inches of water remained, it became obvious that the keel was holed – the water flowed in like a welling spring; but along the V-bottom inside the float was laid an A-shaped girder which made it impossible to see the leak. This girder had round holes punched in it along each side; but they were not large enough to admit more than two fingers. I could only roughly locate the leak by stuffing a rag behind the girder, at the end near the bulkhead. I tried to devise some way of stopping a leak I could neither see nor feel and which was under water (the pump could not keep the bottom dry); it could only be done from outside the floats. So we pulled the seaplane up the slimy bank then lifted the tail and put some coconut husks under the float heels. There were many of these husks, shallow bowls of matted fibre, floating about. Next we pulled the tail down and placed husks under the front of the floats. Each time we rocked the 'plane we placed more husks underneath and raised it an inch or two higher, until it rested on small piles of half-coconuts. Smith insisted on taking an active part, though the mud stuck to everything like liquid chocolate and he was in clean whites – at the start. I worked in a fever of impatience, having told the Japanese authorities I should arrive that day. I washed the mud off the keel-bottom – there was no sign of any hole underneath. But there must be a hole there. I myself had seen the swelling inflow of water. I furiously scratched my head with muddy fingers. I went over the keel inch by inch, but could find no hole whatever.

The only thing to do was to fill the float with water and see where it came out. We did so – *there was no sign of any leak.* We tried every shift we could think of. Finally we launched the seaplane again. It slid off the mud into the river, and I peered into the float. *It no longer leaked.*

It was now too late for me to start, so I put Smith aboard and tried out the machine in a short flight up the river. The float was all right. There was only a slight weep – nothing out of the ordinary.

But next morning exactly the same thing happened again. The water flowed up through the bottom like a spring. I made abortive attempts to locate the hole; and when that failed, to stop it blindly. The bright tropical sun shone down relentlessly on the edge of the mud-bank. Sweat ran off me in streams as I worked in a fever to be off, standing up to my thighs in the river, my feet in slimy mud, my hands and clothes smeared copiously with paint from the floats, with the aluminium finishing-coat, with the black bituminous under-coat, and with lanoline from the freshly-greased wires, turn-buckles, nuts and bolts.

'At this rate,' I thought. 'I shall niggle away the

rest of my life trying to find the leak. For heaven's sake let's *do* something!'

With that I baled out the float as well as I could, clapped on the manhole and took off for Formosa.

## CHAPTER XVI

### OVER FORMOSA

I WAS so contented at finding myself in the air again that within ten minutes the float trouble seemed to have vanished and was forgotten. It was a perfect day, with a flawless sky, strong sunlight and sparkling deep blue sea. 'Too lazy to write,' I logged. 'Rather fun – the idea of Formosa. Don't care a damn what happens – bad mood. Should pass through the centre of that so-called typhoon 100 miles north of here – word must have degenerated.

'Breeze S.S.W. Last half-hour forty-three miles. Bearing of West Babuyan from island alongside Camiguin: –

'By chart, $7\frac{2}{3}°$.

'By compass observation, 7°.

'Variation is 50′ West, therefore bearing by compass should be $8\frac{2}{3}°$; therefore compass deviation on this bearing is $1\frac{2}{3}°$, say 2°.'

Add to observed bearing.

'Babuyan Island has a very barren chocolate cone. Looks as if it throws lava out pretty frequently. Also, cloud on main peak was bluey, as if smoke. No signs of habitation. . . . Second half-hour, forty-three miles. . . . Dates and sultanas. . . . In half-hour (third) forty-one miles. . . . First shark I've seen for ages. . . . Basco, a most interesting looking spot. They say all the houses are made of stone to withstand the wind. No cars. Inhabitants get money by making clothes at home, then taking them to Manila and peddling them. Thousands of little square fields with high walls on top of the hills – too steep elsewhere, I suppose. . . . Thirty-eight miles last half-hour. . . . Pumped petrol for thirty minutes without halt – had not pumped eighteen gallons by then – three hours out, eighty-two miles last hour. Wind west. Autau Su – reminded me of the Riviera; bases of the hills flattened into little ledge fields of about ⅛ acre each. Flew up close alongside the hills behind – big and steep. Picturesque. A large, healthy bird should be able to nest there if he took care his eggs didn't roll off. Villages, clusters of huts like a swarm of ants on a honey smear.'

Autau Su was an island rising over 1,800 feet. Round the hills at the base it was artificially ledged as if hundreds of irregular steps had been cut; all these were cultivated. The village was a solid clump of stone houses with no empty space or garden; the roofs were grey slate, strange after so much thatch. Behind the buildings towered two wireless masts of grey steel lattice. Whereas the previous island has suggested untidy freedom, this place had the look of an old institution. The island was level with the south end of Formosa, forty miles east of it; but I was forbidden to approach the coast for yet sixty-five miles. Neither that nor anything else worried me; the general course since the Philippines had been due north along the edge of the chart, so that the seaplane had been flying off degrees of latitude in fine style, 18°, 30°, 19°, 20°, 21°, 22°, 23°, and had picked up a south-wester breeze which was bowling it along in fine style. Just north of 23° I made the coast of Formosa, which was not so bad as I had expected. It was true that the rock cliffs became in places the edge of a mountainous island, sheer enough to throw a stone into the sea from 2,000 feet up, or so it looked; but at every few miles there was a beach of rocks or a lean bay of flat land. It was curious to see again what looked like a motor-road running either along the base of the cliffs, or, where the cliffs became a precipice, hewn out of the rock face like a tunnel with one side missing. Sometimes I flew within a wing-span of it where it had been forced up hundreds of feet above the sea. With its stone viaducts buttresses and bridges it must have been as costly to make as a tunnel.

On the next flat bay I saw a woman walking; she was dressed in loose black trousers which set off a graceful carriage and easy gait; in fact, she carried herself admirably. My mind switched from road engineering.

I flew over Karenko, the first town or even village I had seen in Formosa. There was a river some distance from it where I might have come down, but I could see no one there or near it, and as I had just enough petrol to reach Tamsui I flew on. The day was still perfect.

At Soo Wan I left the coast to fly across the island. I set the compass on a course of 320°; the distance was only fifty miles.

I now faced a ring of mountains across the Giran

flat, standing up clear against the sky, light brown in the summer sun, with purple shades and distances. I thought that to cross was merely a question of gaining sufficient height to slip over a saddle. I could expect my machine to labour at 5,000 feet, flounder at 5,500, and reach its absolute ceiling at 6,000; but this caused me no anxiety; for no saddle would be anywhere near as high. However, every thousand feet extra would slow the seaplane considerably, so I looked round for the lowest saddle I could find.

I had no map of the mountains; but only my sea-chart, which showed nothing between the coasts but four heights, 11,490 feet south-west of my course, 8,887 west, 3,483 just to the north, and 2,420 well to the north; but these last two were both in the prohibited area. The saddle I chose was about 30° south of my course and between the 3,400 and 8,800 marks. The weather was perfectly fine, and I presumed that the range across my path was a simple backbone, and that once over the divide I should find the west coast stretched before me flat and easy. I fastened my safety-belt securely, climbed steadily while crossing the fifteen miles of plain, and by the time I reached the saddle had nearly 2,000 feet to spare. But instead of the plain I had expected on the other side, I could see nothing but mountains and cloud in every direction. I found myself in a long, narrow-gutted ravine with a mountain torrent below; rock precipice showed bare among the dense green forest that packed the slopes. On my left the mountains towered out of sight in dark cloud; that only made me feel tiny in space; but ahead of me, stretched across the rocky defile from mountainside to mountainside, filling it half-way down to the torrent below, was a sagging black-hearted rain-cloud blocking my path. I hesitated, unwilling to turn back. My orders were to cross south of the Giran-Tamsui line. If I went round the prohibited

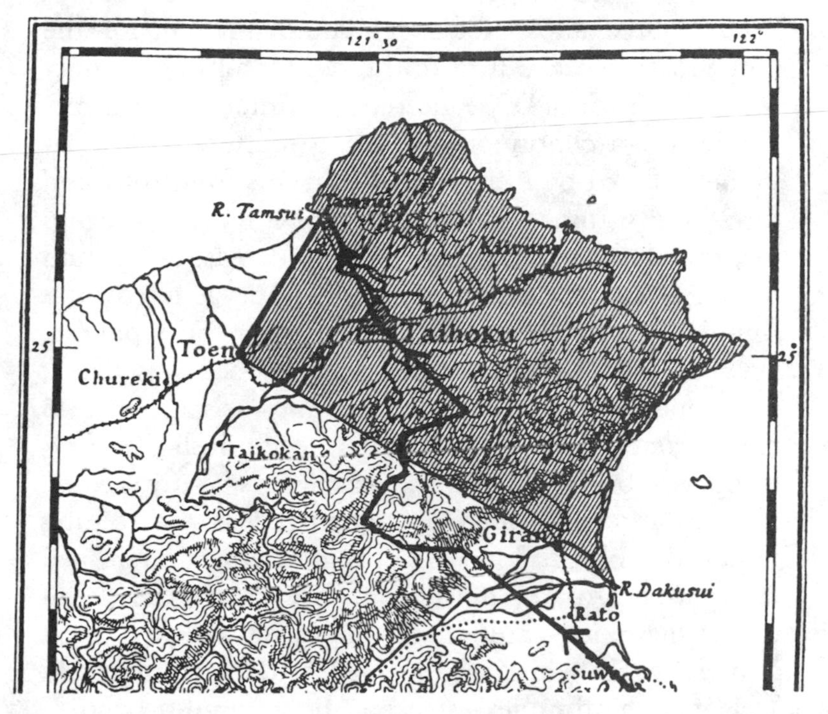


Map of north of Formosa, showing forbidden zone.

north coast, I should be compelled to keep well out to sea and would therefore need to return to Karenko for more petrol. Under the cloud I could see a stretch of river-bed which, with its rocky half-forested sides made a picture in a bright watery-green setting. That showed it must be clear on the other side of the cloud, I thought; and that I could safely sacrifice my height. I closed the throttle and dived under the cloud. I emerged to find myself in a precipitous gorge and was conscious (or imagined it) of the torrent roaring below. 2,000 or 3,000 feet above my head the valley was sealed from range to range by cloud. What waited ahead for me I could not tell, for the gorge made a sharp turn to the right, and I could only see a bleak dark V-section of mountain facing me. There was a continuous whizzing motion of the seaplane buffeted by different air-currents from rock and forest and water. All the time I was trying to regain height. I turned the big bend with ease. I found myself in another reach of ravine. It was filled by a thunderstorm. I felt a bitter hatred for the Japanese. . . . It was as dark as twilight; the rock was black, the slopes looked chill, with tenuous wisps of steam rising from them. For an instant each flash lit everything with brilliant light, but afterwards it only seemed to fall darker. Strangely enough it was not raining under the black cloud. Feeling numb, I sacrificed my spare height and flew under. A flash in the gloom under the cloud-vault made the forest a sickly green and the rocks white. It seemed as dark as nightfall. I cleared the thunderstorm and flew round a bend to find myself in another gorge. And this time it was completely blocked. Time seemed both to race and stand still, for by now the thunderstorm would be down behind me; and I could fly blind through neither thunderstorm nor rain-storm in a rocky gorge. Ahead of me a foggy white cloud was wedged between the sides near the bottom, and under it hung a gauzy opaque curtain of rain. In this the river faded away and was swallowed from sight. I felt paralysed. I must decide instantly what to do – and felt I could not decide. I began to turn, but was afraid in the gorge. I swung back on the course; but that was certain death. I *must* turn; of course I could turn.

As the seaplane went about in a whirling turn I saw the ravine in my mind, with every tree clearly pictured, the falls and boulders in the river, the strange brighter green of its sides just before it was lost in the rain, the cloud ceiling overhead, the little branch valley coming in from the north. . . . Even if the thunderstorm were not yet down I could not climb high enough in the distance to regain the saddle. Wild, bitter rage against the Japanese. . . . I was reviewing the scene behind me. . . . The upstream gully: no, I would try that first. I turned north again and made for it; climbed at full throttle. It was a side valley. With a great tired relief I found it clear. But it climbed up to the cloud ceiling. I kept the seaplane climbing. Presently, close under the cloud ceiling stretched across the top, I could see far to the north as through a narrow level slit over a field of hill-tops and under a flat ceiling of cloud. It was my escape – but straight over the fortifications, right through the middle of the forbidden area; well ( – the – Japanese and their – forbidden area), better to end up in prison than on the rocks of a gorge. Suddenly a saddle opened to view on my left and I saw away through it a flooded plain suspended high in air under the cloud ceiling. I turned with a rough wrench at the controls and shot through. As soon as I was safe

I felt exhausted as if I had just been through a violent storm. . . .

The flooded plain was paddy-field. I rocketed straight over the middle of Taihoku, the capital, low, so that hundreds of Japanese children in some school grounds stopped playing and stared up at me with a sea of round faces.

## CHAPTER XVII

### HIS EXCELLENCY IS PLEASED

TAMSUI was on one side of a wide river full of mud-banks; the opposite side was the flank of a solitary mountain which rose from the water's edge. I had intended to discover the British Consulate first; and, as someone had told me it was conspicuous, I swooped down on an old solid building of stone which dominated the township; but there was no British flag flying from it. Then to my astonishment I saw a number of Japanese flags, spiky red suns on a white field, flying from other places, and I noticed the stone-faced river-bank was crowded with people, while three launches on the crawl in the river were each flying a Japanese flag and full of white-uniformed officials. It gave me quite a shock; Aparri's indifference had put the idea of ceremonious welcomes completely out of my mind. I felt flustered and remembered how fast the water had rushed into my float before I left Aparri. I gave up my search for the Consulate, circled the water, and alighted outside a launch. There was a strong tide or current and all movement on the water seemed fast. The seaplane at once began drifting seawards. The launch rushed up.

'Must anchor in shallow water,' I shouted.

They chattered among themselves.

'My float's leaking,' I shouted.

They seemed to be undecided.

The seaplane was carried into shallow water over a mud-bank in midstream, and I thought I had better anchor there in case the seaplane sank quickly. I hurriedly extracted and rigged my anchor. This seemed to excite the officials. There were cries from them; they talked rapidly among themselves. 'Must anchor in shallow water,' I cried. No one understood, but plainly the sight of my anchor was upsetting them. I let it go and it held with a strong rip of tide at the floats and rope. Another launch full of officials approached and a man on board began introducing them to me, as if I were holding a levee. I was never in my life in such a ludicrous situation. Always irritable immediately after a flight, and with my time-sense changed, impatient of the least delay, I was now in a fever at thought of my float filling under me; while official after official stood up in the launch, was introduced in English of which I could not understand a word, and bowed three times. To make the scene more farcical I was filthy from head to foot with Aparri mud, grease and paint; my kapok-padded jacket which never had much shape at the best of times was now bulging with cord and rags in the pocket; in soft rubber shoes it was impossible to feel dignified even had they not been dirty and shapeless; I had on a dirty shirt without a collar; my hair and beard were tousled; my nails felt separate from my fingers.

Once the introducing had started I could not very

well interrupt them even if the 'plane sank under my feet. I fumed and fretted while the second launch came up and everybody in that was introduced. Sometimes they were within hearing and sometimes out of it – the launches were kept on the move by the current.

Immediately the introductions were over I shouted that I must get the seaplane into shallow water inshore before it sank.

'You will tie up to mooring arranged for you, yes?' asked the English-speaking Japanese.

'My float is leaking; the seaplane is going to sink.'

'There is mooring for you ready.'

'My plane is *sinking*; I must get into shallow water.'

There was great agitation and talk.

'The Customs officer will come to your seaplane now.'

'Can't you put that off till later? I tell you my seaplane is sinking.'

Already I could sense the float under my feet losing buoyancy. A third launch arrived also crowded with officials or reporters, but with the British consul, Ovens, on board. Again I was forced to wait for the introductions to end. Then I cried out to Ovens:

'I've got a leaking float and my 'plane is sinking; I want to get in to the shore at once.'

Ovens was a tall Englishman in a tropical suit of yellow-tinted white and a pith helmet. He had some difficulty in raising his voice to a loud enough shout and seemed rather self-conscious as if he had never before been called upon for anything so undignified, and disapproved either of my dirty self as a fellow-countryman or of the Japanese effusiveness of welcome.

He seemed to find it hard to understand that my needs were urgent.

He said the Customs man wanted to inspect my 'plane and that I had better let him.

I snapped back that it was ridiculous to insist on inspecting the machine immediately, it could be done quite as well after I had been towed into shallow water. They could do anything they wanted to do then.

After a long palaver with them he said he thought it would be advisable for me first to let the Customs official board the seaplane. I groaned. His being the British consul ended my resistance. I said, 'Then they'll have to send across a sampan; that great power-driven launch will only smash up the 'plane.'

In due course a sampan arrived. It was propelled by a small Japanese in a sailor suit with a whistle cord, and a round, unpeaked cap with ribbons streaming from the back, and 'Customs' in gold letters on the band. He looked rather like the principal boy in an opera, but manœuvred his flat-bottomed sampan with amazing skill by means of a strange-looking skull worked to and fro behind the stern; it resembled the blade end of an oar broken off short and spliced to a scythe-handle. When the Japanese came alongside I gave them my Journey Log-book which officials at a port liked to stamp and sign, also my sealed camera, the double-barrelled pistol and its ammunition. My orders were, 'no explosive powder, weapon of war, ammunition and camera are allowed to carry with'; and I thought that my handing them over would make me appear transparently honest, besides that it was amusing to hand over formally such trifles; it was some revenge for their petty red-tape that was endangering my seaplane and their obtuseness to my urgent needs.

'And now,' I said, 'my seaplane has leak in float, has a hole in the bottom, you understand, and is sinking, *sinking*; I must get it ashore at once.'

They conferred and then the interpreter said, 'They will inspect your baggage now.'

'They can inspect my baggage when my seaplane is on shore and not before,' I said, exasperated, 'I tell you my seaplane is sinking.'

I half expected them to turn nasty, but by now did not much care if they did; however, they accepted this and returned to their launch. I think they were excited at being the officials to board the 'plane in front of the crowd. When they reached the launch another conference took place. Then they threw me a line and towed the seaplane to a mooring above the pier. Here the current flowed with such force that the launch could barely make headway. It was the worst position possible; any mistake and the seaplane would be immediately carried into the jetty piles. As they reached the mooring the port float on which I was standing went under water. I jumped across to the other float and shouted to the launch to tow the 'plane in to the beach immediately. They could not – it seemed as if they would not – understand. I could not land until the quarantine officer had been on board and permitted it. Another launch arrived with an Englishman on board; he said he was the A.P.C. representative. I said, 'One of my floats has a hole in it and the seaplane is sinking fast; for heaven's sake get them to run the 'plane ashore before it goes down.'

He understood at once and tried to explain to the Japanese. I fumed while ten of them talked together rapidly. At last I could stand it no longer and cried to the A.P.C. man:

'For God's sake throw me a line, man, and tow me in yourself; I tell you the 'plane is going to sink at any moment.' He looked positively scared at my suggestion. 'No, no, he couldn't do that'; however, he redoubled his efforts at persuasion, and at last his soft, almost timid, way of dealing with the Japanese was successful, the launch towed me in close to the mud shore, a line was thrown and the seaplane secured in shallow water. McKay the representative of the A.P.C. (the Asiatic Petroleum Company, as the Shell Company is named in the East) undertook to have the seaplane carried ashore on bamboo poles and the leak investigated. After a short talk with him about ways and means I went away feeling confident for once that I could leave my work to someone else.

Ovens and I were now compelled to hold each other's hands for a photograph. He was tall beside me; had a long chin, a clipped moustache and scanty hair, and looked sheepish at such a display of hashed-up sentiment; while I, acutely conscious of looking like a tramp, put on a boisterous roughness. When it was finished they shepherded me through the crowd to the Custom-house, to a long bare wooden table with wine-glasses and a bottle of port on it. Standing round we drank the port, and they toasted the foreign aviator. They then began to question me. What was my route? Did I fly over Giran? Over Karenko? Why had I not alighted at Karenko where I was expected? What route had I followed from Aparri? What was the horse-power of my motor? They surrounded me, hissing these and a number of other questions at the interpreter like a circle of cobras. Then they asked, 'at what hour had I left Aparri?' Now I could seldom remember details of time immediately after a flight, and replied, 'Five or six hours ago.'

Then they sank their fangs into me in earnest.

'What time did you leave Aparri?'

'I don't know; five or six hours before I reached Tamsui.'

'The telegram said you left Aparri yesterday.'

'I can't help what the telegram says.'

'You flew over Basco at 11.5 a.m. to-day, the telegram says. Is that so?'

'I dare say.'

'You left Aparri yesterday; you flew over Basco today. Where were you in the interval?'

'At Aparri, I suppose, since I left Aparri to-day and not yesterday.'

'At what hour did you leave Aparri?'

They asked it twenty times, with a different selection of silly questions in between, while I grew more and more irritable; it seemed such an incredibly stupid question; because in the first place, had I spent the night photographing fortifications in South Formosa, the last thing I should do would be to lie about the time I left Aparri, which could easily be checked; in the second place, if there was anything worth spying on, surely it would at least have a guard capable of detecting the presence of an aeroplane.

However, when they started on my route from Giran through the mountains, I became uneasy. Had they been only working up to this all the time? I knew I had been a few miles into the forbidden area when caught by the storm, and imagined that by some extraordinary means they had found this out. Cautiously I said I had flown as straight as I could from Giran to Tamsui *as ordered*, and this I maintained right through. The fact was I had been ordered to fly south of the line Giran – Tooyen – Tamsui. Tooyen was not marked on my chart. I had supposed it to be some place in a line with Giran and Tamsui, and had forgotten all about it. The consequence was that I had really been flying through the forbidden zone nearly all the way.

But I considered I had tried my hardest to carry out their ridiculous orders, and in doing so had only escaped from the gorge by sheer luck; when therefore they kept on putting the same questions time after time about the mountain route, my time of leaving Aparri, and, most stupid of all, the horse-power of my motor, I first grew angry, then, as it seemed to be developing into the 'third degree', something hardened in me; on the chart I could now see the very minute of my leaving Aparri marked and staring me in the eye, but nothing would have induced me to give it and I stuck to my 'five or six hours'. As they kept on repeating the same questions time after time I became convinced they were determined to wear me down till I broke and confessed. A sort of cold rage took me, perhaps childish, but I had had a gruelling day – Aparri in the mud, a 500-mile flight, scared out of my wits in the mountains, the officials, the sinking 'plane, and now this; so that when they next asked me what the horse-power of my motor was, after repeating 100 h.p. till I was sick of saying it, I replied 20 h.p. for a change. The next time I said 25, and from now on added 5 h.p. at every question (the horse-power varied with the revolutions, minimum 20, maximum 100). Doing this amused me and I felt better. Presently I began to answer anything that entered my head and from that I came to bantering them, rallying them, and making poor jokes. In the end they gave me up and handed me over to Ovens, who took me home; he told me it was a very risky thing to rag a Japanese, but by then I had not much cared.

Mrs. Ovens was a delightful, understanding hostess; amiable, kind, good-natured, she did everything she could to make my stay pleasant and restful. She was not long out from England, where they had recently been married, and our tongues were soon wagging hard over reminiscences. She told me, when I inquired about her name that I found in an old book, that her maiden name too had been Ovens. They were first or second cousins, but opposite in character. Tamsui was a lonely consulate for her, with no other European women nearer than at Taihoku, thirteen miles away; yet I envied them their peaceful existence, in a delightful roomy old stone house with a garden, plenty of native servants, lots of books, and time to themselves.

McKay came up to tell me about the float; the plate

in which the drain-plug was set had been fixed with screws instead of rivets, the pressure of water outside had lifted it like a valve and let the water in; but, on raising the float, the water inside had pressed the plate back again and stopped the leak. Besides this, on dragging the seaplane ashore the viscous mud must have helped to cement the leak temporarily. Could he repair it for me? Yes, he had a skilful workman who could do the job; but of course having no duralumin he would be compelled to use steel. I said that could not be helped and I was very much obliged to him.

'How much time could he have for the job?' he asked.

I said I must leave to-morrow because of the typhoon.

Ovens said he knew nothing of any typhoon and sent off to inquire. A weather forecast said, 'No low pressure in the neighbourhood of the Island of Formosa and Shanghai. Fine weather expected between Formosa and Shanghai on the 6th and 7th August.'

'Well,' I thought, 'that typhoon must be a myth. Father Selga could not have known about it in July without the Japanese knowing about it on the 5th August.'

And so I decided to stay at Tamsui the following day. Nor was I sorry; for one thing I was dead tired, and for another I could accept the invitation or command of the Japanese Governor-General to visit him at his palace at the capital, Taihoku; which I thought should be extremely interesting.

In the morning Ovens motored me in to Taihoku past areas planted in tea which at first I mistook for currant bushes in exact rows up and down and across. On the hillside were paddy-fields with rice in every stage of growth; in some fields it was being planted in liquid mud, in others it was being cut by hand like corn. The fields were laid out in steps up the foot-hills, each one slightly above its neighbour in front, the water kept in by means of a parapet wall. The mystery to me was how the supply could be regulated to flow through hundreds of fields without any man-slaughter among the neighbours. The hot, dusty roads and the dust-covered greenery at the side were strange after so much sea and air and wild country.

At the Governor's palace Ovens and I were ushered in to a lofty room with a row of pillars down the middle. The walls were hung with long black tapestries which subdued the light. An interpreter, whom I thought the most obsequious creature I had ever met, went on bowing to the Governor till I feared he would never stop, bringing his hands to his legs each time and sliding them down to his knees. At last he introduced us. His Excellency then sat at a square table, Ovens was placed on his left, the interpreter on his right, and I opposite.

His Excellency watched me for a long time without the least sign of any feeling whatever. His eyes were so small behind the fleshy features, their expression indomitable and relentless. He had a squarish head with bristly hair and a short thick neck. At first he seemed to be the inscrutable Oriental of fiction who would like to torture a detested foreigner every morning after breakfast.

After a long silence he spoke without taking his eyes off me; the interpreter turned and said:

'His Excellency says that he is pleased you reach this country of Formosa with success.'

I waited a while myself before replying, 'You will please thank his Excellency for the honour he does me.'

His Excellency grunted and there was another long silence before he spoke again. As I waited for about half as long as he did before replying, the conversation had not advanced far at the end of a quarter of an hour. Gradually my opinion of him changed; though both his eyes and his features remained absolutely blank of expression, yet I seemed to be aware of his thoughts. At first, for instance, he was curious to know what they looked like, the crazy foreigners who did such things as these flights. 'A crude unpolished lot compared with us, the Japanese,' was his conclusion after summing me up. But in the end I believe he had a feeling of bored weariness with his 'office', and faintly envied me my bit of freedom and fun.

Towards the end I had a bad moment when the interpreter said, 'His Excellency desires to know the horse-power of your motor,' and I only just suppressed a laugh like a sparrow fluttering in my throat before I replied, 'You will tell his Excellency that the horse power of my motor is 80,' that being the figure I had now reached with 5 h.p. rises.

His Excellency clapped his rather podgy hands, a bottle of sweet champagne was silently produced, and a single glass formally drunk. I left under the impression that, given the opportunity and the necessary encouragement, His Excellency the Governor of Formosa might prove to be a sporting old boy.

Ovens then took me to the Chinese consul, to whom the British Ambassador of Peiping had cabled *his* permission for my visit to China. The amiable consul asked me where I proposed touching the China coast, and when I replied, 'Funing-fu', he warned me that I must not on any account have a forced landing or come down anywhere along the section of coast north of it; it was infested with pirates; in fact, every man there was a potential pirate, and a valuable-looking seaplane with only one man to guard it would be an irresistible prize.

For all the rest of the day I was a gentleman of leisure. The gardener killed a snake on the Ovens' lawn, and I discovered at last why my finger had been irritating – a piece of nail-root had survived, had started growing inside the finger behind the flap and could not find a way out. I had to borrow a razor-blade and help it through.

Next morning Ovens said he could not come down to the seaplane, hummed and hawed about some work he must do; but, through having had his support so far, I had grown used to it and felt I could not do without it, so jockeyed him into accompanying me.

When I came to refuel, the seaplane still rested on empty petrol-cases in the mud, and while I stood on the motor pouring in tins of petrol I was under continuous question-fire from some whites come from Taihoku. Consequently I was forced to stifle my petrol-filling curses and mutter absent-minded answers while the Japanese police, Customs and other officers stood round, arms idle, weight on alternate feet. The craftsman finished the repair to the float, and when all my gear was stowed, the police official ceremoniously returned me my camera, pistol, and cartridges, solemnly counting out the cartridges into my hand one by one – thirteen of them.

I was then conducted to a kitchen-table planted in the mud. On it stood the same dozen wine-glasses as before; but meanwhile Ovens had given the show away by telling me they were his, borrowed for the occasion. Across the expanse of muddy water and mud-flats the sunburnt mountainside rose abruptly. The river flowed past a few yards from our feet. Iron stakes had been driven into the mud and a dirty rope fastened to them which kept a square patch select; and here we stood round the table in the hazy sunlight drinking port wine. I felt a playful goodwill towards my inquisitors.

After that was over, a score of coolies lifted the seaplane by means of bamboo poles under the floats. The foreman snatched off a wide-coned straw hat that threatened to puncture a wing; then, sounding their cries like a lot of human swans, the coolies sloshed over the mud and set down their load in the water. They were a good-humoured lot, and with their easy unambitious practical skill, I think they must have been Formosan natives, not Japanese. Several were holding the floats when I started the motor; the slipstream, catching one of the enormous round hats, sent it bowling over the mud; this drew a roar of applause from the men and, looking down, I saw the owner had joined in the laugh against himself – they were good fellows.

But in the river the tide was running fast. Unfortunately the breeze was blowing the same way as the tide, so that when I went into wind to gain air-speed, I went into tide and lost water-speed. I failed upstream and downstream. The baked air seemed to lie on the surface and press it smooth. I moved over close to a mud-bank, hoping the current there would be slack; but it was an equally dismal failure; I could not even get up enough speed to rise the floats on their step.

I switched off the motor; and found the air hot and sultry with no breeze at all under the towering mountain. I felt stifled. The sea! I must get to the sea! Space! Room to move and breathe! Away from people and their eyes! I let the 'plane drift in the current; but instead of moving straight downstream it traversed the river towards the pier. Evidently the big mud-bank deflected the current; I waited patiently for the downstream to catch the seaplane, but it showed no signs of doing so. Evidently here was the explanation of the tide-race at the pier – the whole river was concentrated at that point. Bother! I should have to start the motor again. But I would not until absolutely necessary; I felt so lazy. Hullo! here was one of the launches. It stopped its motor close in front of the seaplane which was drifting tail first. A man on board cried out something. 'I go to sea,' I shouted, pointing seawards. They shouted, I shouted, they shouted. I thought the Japanese word for sea was something like 'mo'. '*Mo!*' I cried pointing; but I only won a blank look. '*Po!*' I tried. '*Ko, To,*' all without success. I subsided philosophically. What could be done with people unable to understand their own language? Then I chanced to look round. Engaged in foolery and watching the Japanese shrug their shoulders, I had not noticed the seaplane carry into the gut of current, and begin bearing down on the pier with rapidly increasing speed; that discovery aroused me enough from my lethargy, but it was the launch which gave me the shock – the second official launch had come out and anchored behind me – right in my fairway. I sprang to life, switched on, turned round and grabbed the propeller blade – to find the first launch right in front of me. I shouted and waved them aside with my arm; one of them in the bows cupped a hand behind his ear and shrugged his shoulders; they chattered to each other.

'Get out of it!' I roared.

'Hah!' cried the Japanese, picked up a rope and pointed to it.

There was no more time to waste; the seaplane, going down tail first, was nearly on to the launch behind, nearly on to the high stem pointed and waiting. I must risk the launch in front.

Clack – clack – clack-clack – clack – the obstinate brute of an engine made not the slightest response. I swung the propeller furiously. . . . It would never occur to Japanese to slip their anchor, of course. . . . It was no good getting flurried. The motor always started quickly when I was cool. I sprang back on to the wing and, bending over the cockpit-edge, opened the throttle slightly. The second launch was close behind the tail. Clack, clack, breathless curses, clack, the front launch moving aside, splutter, clack, roar, off! As I scrambled into the cockpit, I looked back; the launch anchor-chain was only a few feet beyond the tail. I taxied out furiously, then round and seawards. Hot work! I mopped my forehead. . . .

However, there was no good in needlessly heating up the motor, burning precious petrol; I switched off, began to drift, and was just beginning to cool down when the launches came tearing up, an official picked up a rope and pointed to the sea. I would have preferred to drift down, but could not refuse the kindness. . . .

A mile from the bar we entered a small tide-rip. The broken water was ideal. I shouted and cast off the rope immediately. At the same time came a waft of sea breeze. I hurriedly started the motor, jumped in, and opened right up in one stroke. *Elijah* rose from the waves like a flapping swan. I swept round in a wide arc over the mud-banks, flew upriver, turned, flew at the consulate, saluted the Ovens' waving on the flat roof, dived to the water, and saluted each launch as I flashed past. I could see a belch of white steam at the ship-sirens and steam-launches; the noise must have been terrific, but I could hear nothing.

## CHAPTER XVIII

### SHANGHAI INTERLUDE

I SET the compass for Funing-fu, 142 miles across the strait, a course which would take me over the lighthouse island, Tung-Yung, forty-five miles short of China.

To-day I found the sun was behind me – I was reaching higher latitudes, slowly flying north. The weather was perfect with a light breeze. Soon I was out of sight of land; but the sea, which used to give me a cold feeling inside, was now like an old friend with restful soothing company.

An hour after Tamsui Tung-Yung's faint purple outline came in sight, and fifteen minutes later I shot past level with the lamp a few yards away. Five Chinese stood intent on something in a small walled-in yard at the foot of the lamp building. As I drew alongside, they broke out a red and black Chinese flag at the foot of the mast. Up it went jerk, jerk, jerk. I screwed my head round watching them, and the sight of the bunting being twitched up warmed me with an excitement of anticipation of the unknown that lay before me. I keenly regretted having no flag of my own with which to return their salute; the best I could do to show my appreciation was to dip my wings.

I was half a mile beyond before the flag reached the top of the mast and broke out fully, red and black in the breeze.

'Glorious day,' I wrote. 'Glorious life at the moment. Devilish sleepy, but must take care to come down where there is no chance of a pirate or two sneaking up while I snooze.'

Now I was over the mainland of China.

I had become so drowsy that my head nodded; the moisture-laden air was oppressive, hot and close. I must come down somewhere for a snooze; it was absolutely necessary. I began searching the coast for a suitable place. Funing Bay, Tehinkoen Bay, Namkwan Harbour, Tanue Bay, I rejected; they were all crowded with junks and fishing sampans, with black sails and brown sails, or white sails with black ribs. The number was incredible; the whole coast was infested with them and I would never have believed there were so many boats in the world. It was astonishing that a single fish would survive unless these Chinese were extraordinarily bad fishermen. By this time I was growing impatient. If I kept on much longer my drowsiness would pass off in the air, and besides that, the further north along this coast the tamer were the Chinese villages. By now I could see it was impossible to find any bay free from junks. At last by the time I reached Lotsing I decided to come down on it, junks or no junks. It was a big bay nine or ten miles across and I chose the southern end as the clearest. There was a solitary junk there, but I could see no other for several miles, so that if I kept my eye on the one already there I ought to have at least an hour before any of the others could reach me. I shut off, twisted down steeply, skimmed the water to inspect it closely for fishing-stakes or flotsam, circled, came down, bounced off the surface, and finally settled on it, feeling humiliated at the bounce, which I thought must be due to excitement; but which I presently found had been caused by a smooth swell invisible from above. Immediately the seaplane came to rest, every junk in the bay set sail for it; except the nearest, which was behind me to the south and continued on its course; the fact that the junk near me was the only one to hold its course ought to have aroused my suspicions; but I was dull-witted with drowsiness in the heat. I stripped off my life-saver jacket and coat, and scrambled over the machine in order to inspect the position of the junks on every side. My head was full of buzz and the whirr, whirr, whirr of the air-screw turning slowly in the glide down; my body still tingling after the vibration. I lit a pipe and stood on a float idly watching the water lap at my feet. Even bending low to scan the bay now and then was a fag. I could have kept an easier lookout from the cockpit; but it was soothing close to the water in a heat so sweltering that sea and island and land had an unreal glassy look about them. The fleet was approaching rapidly; however, they were probably quite harmless, I thought. Suddenly I spotted a sampan with its sail down and five or six Chinese on board within a hundred yards of the seaplane's tail. Nothing could have cured my drowsiness more effectively; I was astounded at having overlooked it. I threw my coats into the cockpit, jumped across to the other float, switched on and began swinging the propeller, wondering if the motor would jib. But at the third or fourth swing it started and I taxied off seawards. As I dressed again in the cockpit I was surprised to notice that the leading sampan on the north side was now only about 250 yards off; yet when I had first come down on the bay I could have sworn they were scarcely moving. As for the sampan that nearly caught me, I could only conclude that the junk close to the seaplane had quietly dropped it over the side while pretending to take no notice of me, or that I had dozed. As I rose from the bay I roared with laughter, the slipstream catching me in the teeth; even another bump on a swell did not damp my spirits.

But the heat soon did; it was overpowering, and when I saw a black rain-squall to the east I changed course and flew into it. At first it was delicious; but within a few seconds the sea was beaten flat and covered with a layer of spray indistinguishable from the grey downpour. I turned and bolted back the way I had come out of the core; even then I was forced to fly over the sea for ten or fifteen miles, dodging small islands and junks that suddenly loomed up in the murk, the Chinese on board staring, motionless, like stone men, as the seaplane hurtled past in a brief instant before vanishing through the curtain of rain.

After the squall I flew over a hilly coast with a solid little village on every other hilltop looking like a grey-roofed nest of pirates, the stone cots emptying people into the narrow ways to stare up at the seaplane.

Everywhere the hills were spotted with tombs, like cathedral doors fallen back flat into the hillside in a stone faced niche.

With the same engine-roar, in the same blast for hour after hour, the heat was hard to bear, the drowsiness hard to withstand; at last, after failing through cramp at the first attempt, I wriggled out of my kapok jacket; then out of my coat. A breeze from the S.E. sprang up soon after. I climbed to 3,000 feet to obtain greater benefit from it and struggled into my coats again. It was a forgotten pleasure, flying high, bolting from cloud to cloud, swallowed up and disgorged by steamy opaqueness, glimpsing the dirty yellow water of Hangchow Bay below. I set a compass course for Shanghai 150 miles away. The 'plane was scudding along at a fine pace; I could sense it – by the changed note of drumming vibration from the propeller. And on a tiny uninhabited islet below I could see waves of wind chasing each other furiously across the long grass, a sign that it was now blowing at sea level too. Had I known this was the first wind of the typhoon I might not have flown on in weary indifference to everything.

Now I was over a flat mainland, a vast patchwork of tiny cultivated strips in every shade of green and brown, and veined in all directions by waterways of every width from a foot to half a mile.

Now the Whangpu river; but still I flew on, loath to come down from the clouds. Shanghai. . . . Already I had a complete picture of it in my mind; it would be like the coast villages on a large scale, only flat and with a muddy, winding river stuck all over with wriggling sampans. I would dive and joyride down the river to look at this big village. . . .

I found myself flying beside a cliff of solid masonry. The wind, now blowing with considerable force across the river, was broken up by the mass of buildings and the heat rising from the streets. The seaplane, slapped and buffeted by the gusts, rocked and lurched and bumped down the river, crabbing along half sideways in the cross wind. I had to fly with a firm hand, using the controls roughly; but the drift did at least give me an unobstructed view, to one side of the engine, of my fairway and the ship-masts in it. The river certainly was swarming with junks and sampans, as I had expected; but it seemed to be even more crowded with steamers and warships, mostly gunboats, strung together stem to stern between great iron buoys; the neat little warships in grey or pale blue looked tiny beside the steamers. I glanced at the thousands of people in a continual stir along a wide street open to the river, but could not see anyone so much as look up at the seaplane. I bumped along for another ten miles to Woosung at the mouth of the river. Here the wind was stronger and though blowing across the river, raised a sea in half its width. Tossed about like a leaf, I circled the mouth; but could see no flagged buoy. I returned to the first bend where a fleet of junks was anchored in open formation. There was nothing there either. The only thing I could do was to pick a stretch of water, come down, and take my chance. Then I noticed a tattered dribble of steam at the siren of a launch, dived to it, saw someone wave, flew round again, saw several men standing on the deck with that air of detachment of people waiting and expecting, and put the seaplane down near by with a firm hand. The gusts made taxi-ing unpleasant; one gust, if it caught the 'plane broadside on, would be enough to tip it over. Drifting rapidly, I was already some distance from the launch before I had my anchor down. The launch, or small tug that it was, came at me.

'Keep away,' I shouted through cupped hands.

'Whaat?'

'Keep off!' I roared; white water from the screw was churning about my floats.

'Hey?'

'Keep off! Wreck the seaplane.'

'Whaaat?'

'Send a sampan.'

'Whadyousay?'

'Sampan. S-A-M-P-A-N. SMALL BOAT.'

'He wants a sampan,' someone said in an ordinary voice which I could hear quite plainly.

They drew off and with much arm-waving attracted a strange-looking craft alongside them. It was like the hull of Noah's ark, a wooden antique with a high raised platform at the square stern, and looked more suitable for ferrying elephants than boarding my seaplane. Its sole occupant was an old crone with wisps of hair streaming in the wind. She stood on the stern platform wielding a bent scull, long and heavy, with the end above her linked by a piece of rope to a ring in the platform. First she pushed the middle of the rope away from her with one hand and the scull-handle after it with the other; then pulled them back in turn, the rope creaking, the oar straining. She looked like a witch in a gale twisting a one-stringed harp to and fro.

A white man jumped into this craft from the launch and with dramatic gestures encouraged the old woman to make for me. He was dumpy and thick-set, with an untidy mop of long black hair and no hat. He appeared to be excited, as if I were a drowning man. The sampan came straight for the seaplane, with a thirty-mile wind behind it, and the old woman's oar. Now I took this man for a high official in the Chinese government; therefore when he came within hail and I began shouting that his sampan was too big to approach downwind, I did so politely. But at my every fresh shout he only seemed to urge the old woman with increased fervour. Bang! the sampan struck the float-tip end on. The prow scraped past, and in spite of my pushing against it with all my strength, fetched up against the wing-root. A coolie who had jumped into the sampan with the white man, seized a boat-hook, and jabbed at the leading edge of the wing. Fortunately the boat-hook was within my reach; I struck it aside. The stern of the sampan caught the wind, and swung round broadside-on to the wing. I saw dirty brown claws clutching the ribs in the leading-edge. At the same time I was aware of the old woman's cheery smile, that it had never faded, and that her steady efforts with the big oar had never ceased; the coolie handed off the wing, the sampan drifted past and astern.

I mopped my brow. Little damage done – a lucky escape. Well, now the man would realise the necessity for coming up astern. But to my consternation back he came to the front as fast as he could.

'Can't stay here,' he shouted with such a dictatorial air that I could only asume he was at least a white mandarin. 'You're right in the way of shipping; have to move you.'

Without taking the slightest notice of any remonstrance of mine, he made the old woman work the sampan across my anchor rope; the coolie fished it from the depths with his boat-hook, and they lifted my anchor. How the old woman could manage the sampan by itself was a mystery to me; now she had the seaplane as well, and it took a man's utmost strength to pull against the seaplane's anchor-rope in a strong wind. She stuck gamely to her oar, but we drifted back steadily until right in the shipping fairway. At the beginning I had asked the white man, begged him, implored him to drop my anchor; but he only sprang about excitedly, waving his arms and totally ignoring me. However, at last he was forced to realise that we could only end up on the opposite shore; he dropped my anchor and returned to the launch, leaving me right in the shipping fairway where large steamers seemed to be passing in endless succession, creating a strong wash behind them.

Presently he returned and came at the seaplane from one side. I could do nothing; the continued strain on my throat, of shouting in the strong wind, was too much for it; my voice suddenly died away to a whisper. There was a rending of fabric as the prow punctured the wing-tip.

'Can't stay here,' he cried, 'shipping – dangerous – not allowed.'

He brushed the hair aside from his face and hopped about in the sampan. The coolie with his boat-hook again picked up my anchor rope, the launch backed to the sampan and cast a line. The mandarin tied it to the anchor-rope, using a number of granny knots. The launch took my anchor aboard and moved off at full speed across-wind. The seaplane, though pulled from the side, was weather-cocking so strongly into wind now, that it glided forwards until broadside on to the stern of the launch. The toe of the float to which the rope was secured began to twitch under the strain. I rallied my voice for some last yells; no one took any notice. I can only assume that my continued shouting at the sampan without effect had made them think it some kind of New Zealand war-cry that I always gave on reaching a fresh country. Fortunately my light anchor-rope snapped.

Now I drifted back without an anchor; but the launch chased me and threw me a line. And with the mandarin out of the way I parleyed effectively with them while the smell of their burning oil blew down on me; they returned my anchor, promised to go dead slow and began to crab the seaplane towards the fleet of junks; while every time the wing started to lift at a gust I ran out along it to keep it down with my weight. At last we were out of the fairway and somewhat sheltered among the junks.

'Come aboard,' they shouted.

The white mandarin immediately began exhorting his crew with flambuoyant gestures, his hair streaming in the wind, to bear down once more upon the sea-plane. Straight down-wind he came. Again I tried to shout but my voice failed. With a hole in the fabric, the wing tip buckled, and several ribs in the leading-edge smashed (and lucky to escape so far with that amount of damage) I had had enough of him, mandarin or no mandarin. When he came close, 'You — ' I said, shaking my fist, 'if you barge into me again with that — old ark, I'll wring your — neck!' He listened all right this time. 'What d'you want then?' he demanded. 'Come up from behind you, you — fool,' I said, as the sampan struck. Fortunately the old woman's skill was marvellous; with my frantic shove from the float, the sampan passed round the wing with only a light blow on the tip. In the flurry my hat blew off and went bowling over the water, At last he came up from behind, the old woman managing it with ease. I jumped aboard quickly and snatched the coolie's boat-hook out of his hands, to stop his jabbing at the tail-plane.

'And now,' I said, 'perhaps you will tell me who I've had the honour of dealing with all this time?'

'Yes, of course, I represent the *North China Daily News*, and this,' he said on board the launch, 'is Colonel Thoms, Commander of the Shanghai Volunteer Corps who has come to welcome you to the fair land of the lotus. He also hails from that tight little island New Zealand. I am a South African, and a bit of a globe-trotter like yourself, and a keen airman. This is the China-Police officer who wants to see your papers immediately. I should accede to his request if I were you. It is really most – '

'What am I to do with my 'plane?' I asked Thoms.

The A.P.C. man, Palmer, suggested that they could tow me under the lee of the bank. 'But it's going to be difficult to guard it down here,' he said, 'and it takes an hour and a half to get down by launch.'

'Why didn't you motor down and use a sampan?'

'You can't motor anywhere in China,' said Thoms. 'In the first place there are no motor roads and in the second it's not safe to leave the town. This is China, you know.'

In the end it was decided that I should fly up river to the A.P.C. store and jetty, half-way back to Shanghai. The old woman, her withered face wreathed in a friendly smile, returned me my hat; she had been off by herself and rescued it while we talked.

I drew Palmer aside. 'Look here,' I said, 'can't you come instead of that chap? It's pure luck I've kept my 'plane intact against him. Why didn't you come before?'

'I didn't like to, because he's a flying man himself and none of the rest of us know anything about it.'

Palmer seemed to talk Chinese as easily as a native, and I was back on the 'plane quickly without any trouble. I did not accept his offer of a tow, but said I would drift back until I had the full width of the river for a take off.

'I think I'll come with you,' the reporter said; but I declined his invitation with thanks.

There was a strong tide flowing up-river and, by the time the seaplane neared the far bank of jagged stone behind a row of wooden piles projecting two feet out of water, it had been carried upstream till it faced the most crowded part of the junk-fleet; thereby shortening my run by half the river-width. The only thing I could do was to taxi as much cross-wind as I dared until opposite the opening in the junk-fleet where the launch waited. The waves rocking the 'plane and the consequent danger of the wind catching the lifted wing made it too risky to cross at much of an angle; so that by the time the seaplane was opposite the launch, it was back alongside it. This left only about 200 yards of water to the shore. Exasperated by the constant apprehension of being capsized in the wind, and by the succession of happenings, any one of which might have destroyed the seaplane, had not my luck held good (my motor had jibbed again till close to the stone river-bank), decided to risk it and take off in the water before me. Though I knew it would have been suicide in ordinary weather, I decided that I could do it in the strong wind. . . .

But my heart was in my mouth till the seaplane rose thirty yards short of the bank. Bumping hard in the air over the land, I flew round in a circle, as it is said a man returns to the scene of his crime, to look at the position from which I had taken off. There was not 200 yards of water there; but only 160 or 170 I judged. So staunch little *Elijah* must have taken off in about 140 yards. . . .

I flew up-river until I spotted the store with 'Shell' painted on it, waited circling for a steamer to pass, alighted directly to leeward of the jetty, taxied straight up to it, and cast anchor.

It was comparatively sheltered there. The seaplane

was hauled up on a grass bank beside the jetty, and each wing tied down to oil-drums full of water.

It was dark when we reached Shanghai and trod across a number of sampans to a jetty of pitch black shadows. 'Keep together,' said Thoms. 'They have a habit of sticking a knife into people here and holding the body under water till all is quiet.'

I followed his advice to the letter and stuck close to Thoms himself – he was a big, tall man with a cast-iron constitution and every inch a soldier. No one in their right senses would try to knife *him*, even in the dark.

We reached a road where my luggage was dumped and we stood interminably while I tried to keep the reporter from sitting on the bundle containing my one suit. It was all rather confusing; but apparently we were in China whereas our destination was the International Settlement. Thoms, after a long parley between Palmer and the guard of the petrol store, who stood with loaded rifle behind gates of thick iron grill, was allowed in to use the telephone. Later he emerged mopping his brow and said, 'Palmer, will you try to get that infernal garage? I can't make that infernal operator understand plain Chinese.'

In the end Palmer secured a car, and we started off again; this time through the lighted city. I used to think London crowded, but it was like a provincial town by comparison with Shanghai. The whole place was swarming like a nest of ants – white-clothed, brown-faced vertical ants in a glittering nest. I thought the well-to-do Chinese girls looked most attractive, sitting up straight in their rickshaws, in

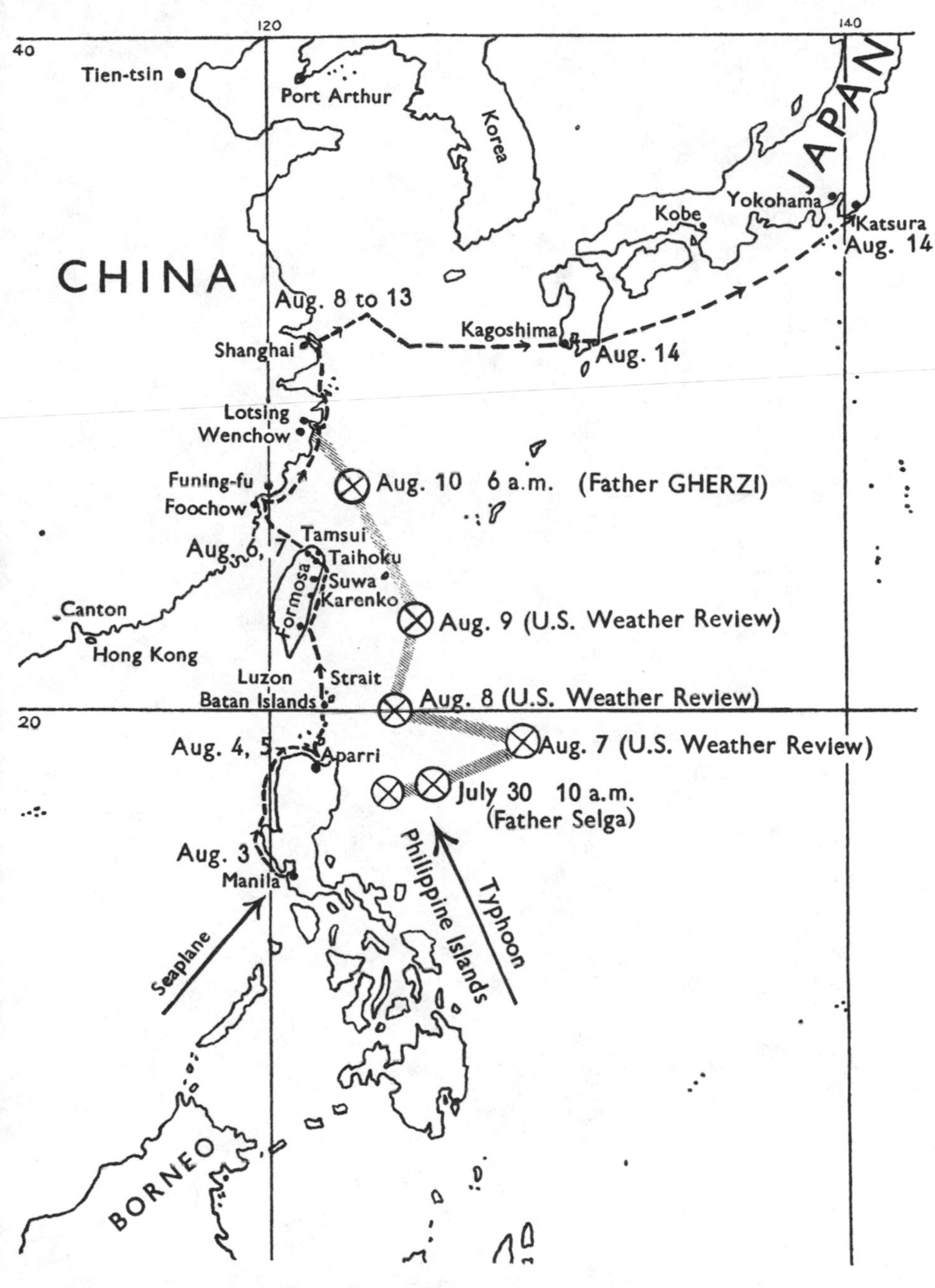


THE COURSE OF THE TYPHOON

black, high-collared jackets, their glossy black hair coiled tightly on either side of the neck, and their smooth, sallow faces with narrow slanted eyebrows.

I said to one of the petrol men, 'Isn't this the place that Ulysses had such difficulty in passing, because of the sirens.'

'No,' he said, 'I don't think he passed here; if he did, he wasn't using our petrol.'

Colonel Thoms, D.S.O., M.C., was a New Zealander and had the typical erect figure of the professional soldier. He had seen a great deal of service and was at the Staff College in England when appointed to the command of the Shanghai Volunteers. He seemed to me the ideal soldier; impossible to shake out of his coolness, a man who quietly summed up every situation (he presented me with a new anchor-rope next morning that would have held a steam launch), and who assessed every street, open place, or block of houses, for the use he could make of it in defence or attack. The only trait not expected in such a man was an easy flow of talk. He took me to a pleasant modern brick house such as can be seen in any rich colonial suburb, only that it was well walled in and had neighbours similarly walled in. In the morning he apologised when I asked him about some shots which had woken me twice during the night. 'I ought to have told you,' he said, 'that in Shanghai you turn over in bed and go to sleep again when you hear shooting. It is usually the armed bodyguard of some wealthy Chinese merchant repelling an attempt to kidnap their employer. There are other scraps too. Nothing of any importance.'

My first task was to ring up the Observatory for a weather report. Crossing the China Sea was a 538-mile flight, seven hours for my machine in still air. There was no land between the two countries so I had no intention of taking off without forty-five gallons on board, nine hours fuel; but even so a twenty-mile breeze against me would lengthen the flight to nine and a half hours, in other words, force me down half an hour short of Japan.

The Observatory was at a Jesuit Convent, Siccawei, which unfortunately was not in the Settlement. When, after great difficulty, I got them on the telephone, I could not understand their English nor they my French. As I must have a weather report I set off for the convent in Thoms's car.

The whole of that day I spent in travelling by car, on foot, or in a launch. The drive to Siccawei in Thoms's car with his Chinese boy chauffeur was exasperating; we hooted our way yard by yard through narrow alleys barely wide enough; with cries from the coolies, jingling of rickshaw bells, and native chatter, continually in our ears; lucky to run ten yards without the human swarm closing round us and checking our way or forcing the car to stop with a jerk. I doubt if we made a mile an hour. But at last we reached Siccawei, a deserted old-world garden, with green grass and mossy stone-flags; and I waited in cool, silent stone halls while a priest went to find Father Gherzi.

Father Gherzi was a tall thin man well over six feet, with black hair, a narrow black beard and a slender high-browed head. He wore a long black robe, and from under it projected two enormous black boots. Quick-gestured, impatient, impetuous, clever, hard-working, he had as much sympathy with a fool as a ferret with a rabbit; was as patient under opposition as a lynx under a whip-lash. When he said something in his rapid, emphatic way it was a fact; but I, who had had a lesson from the reporter only the day before about taking emphatic men at their face value, cross-examined Father Gherzi after he had told me about the weather; and so he thought me a fool. Yet how could I expect to find a great meteorologist in Shanghai in a black gown? And also it was not easy to follow him. I could understand his French better than his English, but did not like to insist on it for fear of offending him. He said there was a typhoon centred to the east of Formosa, that it was travelling fast and coming straight for Shanghai, that it was impossible for me to leave for Japan because a thirty-five mile wind was blowing from the E.S.E. (right in my teeth), and that I must secure my seaplane at once.

I left Siccawei thoroughly scared for my machine out on the mud in the open; rushed back to Thoms's office; from there with him to the Shanghai Club to look for the Air Force Intelligence officer, and find out where I could shelter my seaplane. The long narrow bar of the Club ran like a straight lofty passage deep into a building, and was full. The number of suggestions I received for safeguarding the 'plane, and the ease with which they were given, was astonishing. An ex-navy man suggested putting it in a floating-dock; an ex-army man taking it to the Town Hall on a lorry (unfortunately there was no road to where it was), and Paddy Fowlds, ex-R.A.F., flying it up to Peiping (Pekin). I gathered that the night life at Peiping was something to marvel at; also that Paddy Fowlds would be delighted to act as observer on the trip. As a matter of fact, to fly north immediately would have been the best thing I could have done; but I was weary to the bone, had the idea of flying to Japan fixed in my mind, could not admit a fresh idea of flying in a different direction. At last Palmer suggested I should ring up Daly; he was the R.A.F. Intelligence officer, and proved it by curtly asking whether I had tried the seaplane hangar. Seaplane hangar? Yes, there was a North China Aviation Company which maintained an air service inland, and had a big hangar beside the Whangpu, with a concrete apron (slipway).

I rushed off to their office, but unfortunately it was a half-holiday and everyone had left, except a Chinese in horn-rims, who could get no answer when he telephoned the hangar (they had a direct wire to it, I think), and who knew nothing about aeroplanes; but he assured me I should be welcome at the hangar. From there I went to the A.P.C., who lent me a launch; then I set out with Palmer to find the hangar.

Strangely enough, out of the wind and in the lee of the deck-house, I could bask in a hot, though hazy sun which still shone and gave the typhoon an air of unreality; and I should have enjoyed the trip up-river, had not my skin felt like dried peel.

In due course we reached the hangar; found the concrete apron on a lee shore and the wind blowing with full force on to it at an angle; and instead of being closed up for a half-day, the hangar looked as if it had been sealed up for ever. The only man there was a Chinese soldier who stopped marching up and down with a fixed bayonet to stare hard at us.

My heart sank at the prospect of unsealing the hangar, of finding and inducing Chinese to make a launching cradle, of organising them into a launching crew, and finally of trying to cradle the seaplane on a lee apron in a strong oblique wind, without smashing it to little pieces. The seaplane was safer where it was out in the open.

While we debated, the launch drifted aground and stuck in the mud. A sampan rammed us amidships and drove us on further. The natives raised shrill cries. The launch churned up a wash of mud. Now we were off. But another sampan barged into the stern and put us aground again. In the end the launch swivelled round in the current, cannoned into a junk, and was under way, leaving an angry buzz behind.

That evening Paddy Fowlds invited me to his birth-day-party. After dinner we went to Luna Park, rode on merry-go-rounds, shot with rifles which, I am convinced, fired bullets on a corkscrew course, and gambled at housee-housee, a game which you lose with the constant expectation of winning; but I most enjoyed watching four Japanese play miniature golf under the garish electric light; they were as serious and concentrated on their game as if it were a matter of life or death; each uttering a short, sharp 'Hah!' when he hit the ball, and drawing breath through his teeth with a hiss each time the ball struck an obstacle – which it invariably did.

I was willing to try anything except one horrible machine with long chains dangling from the top and a chair at the end of each chain, which spun out into the air as the thing revolved, and which I knew would make me airsick.

Soon only Paddy and I were left of the party, and it was five o'clock in the morning before we had sufficiently plumbed the depths of Shanghai's pleasure life. I went to bed with the sensation that life was used up, that I had no more left, and that in any case there was nothing to live for.

Next day, August 9th, Father Gherzi looked worried. He said nothing about the typhoon destroying 2,000 houses in the Ryukyu Islands, east of Tamsui that morning – probably he did not know about it yet – but, with abrupt sentences, he told me it looked as if the typhoon were going to curve to the east of Shanghai, that it was gathering speed, and that I *must* make my machine secure. But how was I to do that? A city of all those inhabitants and nowhere to shelter a small seaplane! Not that that mattered much now – already the wind made it too risky to manœuvre.

I went down to the seaplane, pulled her further up the mud, and raised the float-heels on blocks so that the wind would rather press the wings down than lift them up. What could I do? I could not fly the China Sea against a half-gale, I could not fly west inland, I could not fly south into the heart of the typhoon. As for flying north, I shrunk from the tedious negotiations it must entail and in any case I might be no better off, for the typhoon was likely to chase me there. I racked my brains for a solution. It was fantastic that I could find no shelter in the whole city. But now nothing on the lee side of the river – not the best equipped of seaplane hangars – could help me. The only shelter I would dare to try for was a building open to the water on the windward side of the river, and where I could taxi straight up to it against the wind: I could find no such place. My little seaplane must stay where it was, on the mud out in the open, exposed. . . .

On the way back I called at the semaphore tower on the Bund, where Father Gherzi attended every afternoon; but he had already left. I had achieved nothing all day. Next morning it was the 10th, the day the *Waishing* was wrecked in Namkwan Harbour a few miles south of the bay where I had alighted on my way up the coast, and the *Kwongsang* went down with all hands at Funing-fu, my landfall of three days before. I did not know this at the time; Shanghai seemed to be walled off from the rest of the world; it was a mystery to me how Father Gherzi obtained the data necessary for plotting the typhoon's course as accurately as he did. He told me it was centred at about Lat. 27 North, Long. 123 East, and appeared to be curving to the west of Shanghai instead of to the east; but that was an unusual curve for August and it was likely to recurve and make directly for Shanghai.

A typhoon is inexorable when you are waiting, waiting, waiting, following its steady approach, standing in its danger. This one had travelled 360 miles yesterday – fifteen miles an hour day and night, fast for a typhoon. Father Gherzi expected the wind to increase to fifty miles an hour that afternoon. I decided that if he fired the typhoon gun, I would go down to my seaplane and stand by it all night. Possibly there might be something I could do when the time came.

At four-thirty the typhoon gun was fired, and I went off down the river in the launch to my seaplane, revolving the problem endlessly in my brain.

Presently I had a faint stirring of hope; when the seaplane flew at 100 miles an hour it was in a wind of that speed. Could I not, therefore, arrange somehow for it to be in the typhoon wind without hurt? Such a wind passing over the wings gave the 'plane a lifting power equal to about a ton's weight. If therefore I weighted the 'plane with a ton of water in the floats, why should it not ride out the wind? If only the 'plane could be kept facing the gale, I believed it could do it. . . . Unfortunately when the floats were full of water I should be unable to shift the 'plane round to face the wind. Well, I must simply load the 'plane and wait. . . .

I had *Elijah* pulled under the lee of a wall and tied down by the wing eyebolts to full oil-drums; then removed all the bilge plugs so that when the tide rose the floats would fill with water – my floats, their interiors beautifully white enamelled, full of that filthy water!

The caretaker put me up for the night in the two-cabin house-boat in which he lived. He was an Englishman who had served his time in the China customs, and told me some interesting stories of Chinese 'squeeze'. As some men dream of the door opening to admit a beautiful strange princess in scanty attire, so I think that by night this man dreamt of Chinese merchants approaching meekly with a ponderous bag of silver dollars up the sleeve, and by day he dreamt of his power to turn them off the wharf, if he wished. He was an edgy fellow to mix with, as a result of living alone, I think; rooted in his opinions; and with a shell to protect him from being touched by anyone else's feelings, due perhaps to long association with Orientals.

Every time I awoke the wind was blowing unchanged in force; and in the morning it was still the same, no stronger, no weaker. Suddenly I thought, 'What a weak fool I am to be sitting here like a paralysed rabbit waiting for the typhoon to catch me! Then I had an idea.

I returned to Shanghai by the first launch that called and at once sought out Father Gherzi.

He said the typhoon had struck the coast at Wenchow (Lotsing Bay, where I had alighted among the junks) and was moving inland, but he expected it to curve northwards and make for Shanghai.

I told him then that I intended leaving Shanghai in the morning, typhoon or no typhoon. I had worked it out; a wind that would prevent my reaching Japan would blow me towards Korea. If, after five hours over the sea, I took a sextant sight and found I had not enough petrol to reach Japan, I would turn north, fly with the wind and make Korea. Even with a sixty-mile wind against me from the S.E. I could do this. It was all very simple.

Instead of ordering me not to leave as I had

expected, Father Gherzi said, 'Very well,' and then begged me not to, until he had reports in from Korea and Japan in the morning. . . .

How could I possibly wait for the reports? I must leave Thoms's house at dawn to reach the seaplane by seven o'clock and be ready to take off by nine. And the trip from the oil store to the city took hours; so that I could not return by launch for the reports and leave the same day; lastly, there were no telephones or roads to the seaplane.

However, Father Gherzi had put it as though it were a personal favour to him; so that I should just have to devise some plan for communicating with him, that was all. It seemed to me that Paddy was the only solution of the difficulty. Paddy fell in with the idea, and it was arranged that he should see Father Gherzi, that I should fly back up the river, and that he should signal to me with flags from the top of the A.P.C. building; if the weather were favourable below 5,000 feet, one flag; above, 5,000, two flags; too dangerous for me to leave, three flags.

I returned to Thoms feeling joyful at the thought of action; but Daly, the R.A.F. Intelligence officer, took the wind out of my sails by asking me why I had not flown my 'plane to the seaplane hangar. I told him. That hangar, he said, was the Chinese Army's; the American company's hangar was further upstream. When I had recovered from this piece of news I went down to the Company's office. They said they had waited for me at the hangar on Saturday, that they had a skilled launching crew, and a proper Moth cradle, relict of their own Moth seaplane. . . .

In the morning, after the comprador of the petrol depot had painted 'a fair wind and an easy voyage' on the fuselage in Chinese characters, I let the seaplane drift across the river, which it did very fast, and then took off with the greatest ease. I had forty-eight gallons on board and could have lifted sixty in that wind, I regretfully decided.

The seaplane scuttled up the river; it was a wonderful relief to be in the air again, and unaccountably soothing to fly with a strong wind; hard to realise that when I turned round I should be flying against it.

I could not at once pick up the A.P.C. from the row of buildings all so much alike along the river-front; until I found the semaphore tower like a tall pillar at the riverside, and worked backwards from that. Ah! there! flags – there seemed to be flags on every building for miles. . . . But what was that? Surely that could not be three flags in a triangle! Impossible. . . . But it was. . . . Three flags. And after taking-off so easily with a full load! I was disgusted at everything.

I let the 'plane fly on up-river.

Well, at least I would alight at the Company's hangar. And it seemed like child's play, landing the seaplane with a proper cradle and an expert crew, up smooth concrete. The wind was less at ground level, the day was close; I had a blank feeling about everything except hunger. I had been up since dawn. I sat in the cockpit and devoured the provisions intended for the China Sea. I felt angry with Paddy for stopping me; but only in a trivial, unmeaning way: I rang him up. 'Quite impossible, my dear chap, quite impossible. Father Gherzi said there was a sixty to seventy-mile wind against you. Sheer suicide.'

Having free time and the seaplane on firm land, I took the opportunity of inspecting the fuselage closely. The fabric was peeling off the underside, the plywood beneath looked sodden. That meant that the glue had gone. And the fuselage was only made of plywood glued on to a thin wooden skeleton, and of fabric glued on to the plywood. The glue was the chief strength of the aeroplane. And now that the glue was rotting, the aeroplane must break up soon; a good buffet from a gust would break off the tail. It was never built for this work, of course. I wished, as I tore off the useless fabric, and covered the three-ply with black bituminous paint, that I had a parachute. But somehow nothing mattered greatly.

One of the Americans gave me a lift back at lunch-time, and once more I was threading the narrow streets choked with coolies. The Thoms were just as hospitable; but I felt vaguely out of place, ineffective. I had turned up again after leaving.

In the afternoon I went into the city to confer with Father Gherzi. This time he was adamant; I must not leave in the morning before he had at least the Japanese reports at 8.30 o'clock. That would mean a 9.30 start, a frightful hour for starting a sea-flight to a strange country; but what could I do with a gentleman who insisted on safeguarding me to his utmost? There was something essentially fine about that dark, impatient man; one left him with an impulse to live a better life.

Later, returning from the French Club with Paddy,

I saw a strange sight; eight little Chinese maidens on a wheelbarrow, four on each side, backs against a rail down the middle, legs dangling inertly, like Chinese girl-effigies. They were going home in their hackney wheelbarrow, factory girls who had clubbed together and hired it for the season.

Next morning, with the Thoms's second-best chicken in a paper-bag, I set off once more. It was the 13th of the month. I kept on telling myself that a superstition was absurd, unless one had enough faith in it to set one's instinct trying to make it come true. 'Since you *do* believe in this one superstition,' urged a voice in me, 'that is the very reason why you should not attempt this flight to-day?' 'Rubbish! 13 is a lucky number for me, not unlucky; I left Wellington on a 13th, arrived in Sydney on a 13th, flew solo for the first time on a 13th, and to-day I'm leaving Shanghai on a 13th.' 'These thirteens are repeated omens of disaster!' 'I don't care what they are; I'm flying this sea to-day. I'm not going to be the slave of any damned superstition.'

'Yes,' said Father Gherzi, 'you can leave to-day. And yet the conditions are not so favourable. You will have a wind against you for a considerable distance from the S.E. or S.S.E., force 6 Beaufort. Possibly at 5,000 feet, this might change to a favourable westerly, but by misfortune of losing the balloon in a cloud it is not certain. At Kagoshima the wind can be expected force 0 or 1.'

After checking my watch with correct Greenwich Mean Time, ready for sextant work when half-way across the sea, I left for the hangar, Thoms's boy driving.

To leave for the hangar and to reach it proved very different matters. We ended up in a *cul-de-sac* before the gates of some large closed factory. The boy set off to make inquiries. After about twenty minutes he returned leisurely and tried by signs to induce me to follow him through some backyards to the river. Certainly the river was in that direction, but looked to me a considerable distance off, judging by the masts which rose from a landscape of vegetable-plots, back yards and pigsties. I was suspicious, knowing what a peculiar sense of direction and distance some people have; but what made me more suspicious was that I could not see the wind-sock which should be visible, blowing from the top of the hangar. For all I knew, this young Chinese might have an aunt living near by, whom he had not visited for months. . . . I refused to leave the road, and re-entered the car. He set off again, we reached a village, and he made more inquiries. It seemed to me, watching, that no one there knew of this Lungwha hangar; that the Chinese did not concern themselves with anything outside their immediate environment. Off we went again. Suddenly we met a car coming from the *opposite* direction as it flashed by I recognised a Chinese in it; I had seen him at the hangar. I tapped on the boy's shoulder, and gesticulated excitedly. The idea of a chase seemed to appeal to him; he turned and set off wildly after the car, swinging round corners, dodging coolies at times, losing sight altogether of our quarry. I was beginning to wonder how we should discover our position if this proved a wild-goose chase; when suddenly I spotted the hangar in the distance.

A few minutes after we had arrived *Elijah*, all ready for the flight, was in the water. I started the motor and, as I taxied up-river to warm the engine and oil, I made certain that everything was at hand in the cockpit; sextant, slide-rule, nautical almanac, log-tables, watch, barometer, log-book, charts, drawing-instruments. There was still a high wind and *Elijah* slipped easily off the water.

## CHAPTER XIX

### DRIFT

I TURNED as soon as I had height enough above the Whangpu River, headed for Japan, set the compass on a course nearly due east – 1° 5′ north of east – and started to climb in search of the favourable westerly, which Father Gherzi had predicted at 5,000 feet. Climbing as high as that meant seriously slowing down the 'plane during the climb and a further loss in speed in maintaining the height when I reached it. But a single glance at the land sidling underneath was enough to drive me up – the seaplane was drifting 30° in the strong south-easter against it, and for every mile I flew towards Kagoshima at that level, I was being carried half a mile away to the north.

At 3,000 feet I passed through a belt of dirty-white clouds massing together, which blew tepid and opaque into my face; down between them I could see the flat dull land as though glimpsing into great depths.

From this height I made out the drift to be still 25°; therefore the wind against me had dropped very little so far; however, I climbed on, always hoping to reach a favourable wind a few feet above.

Through a break in the cloud-floor I saw the southern end of a flat mud island. I took it for Drinkwater

Point on Tsungming Island, and wrote that the seaplane had drifted 45° so far.

Actually it was House Island 13 miles to the south and a considerable distance nearer Shanghai.

Calmly considered, this seems an incredible mistake, after I had observed the drift to be 25° and written it down in the log only a few minutes before. But it had been such a relief to feel that I had really shaken myself free from Shanghai at last, and escaped the typhoon, that a reaction had set in and I had sunk into a kind of apathy concerning everything.

It is true that House Island was not plain on the chart among all the sand-banks, beacon spots and soundings, and that it was difficult to see much of the island down the cloud chimney, but a moment's reflection ought to have shown that I could not have flown the distance to Tsungming in the time.

The result of this mistake was that I flew on quite contentedly without realising that the speed of the plane was too slow for it to reach Japan. It was only making fifty miles an hour against the wind and not even in the direction of Kagoshima; but towards a point 250 miles north of it. At the speed the 'plane had made as far as House Island it would take me eleven and a half hours to reach Japan, whereas I had started with only nine hours petrol.

So dull-witted was I, that when presently I flew over another island out to sea and could not find it anywhere on my charts, I still did not suspect my mistake. And wrote in my log 'Flew over unknown island, 4,000 feet, 2.4 Greenwich Mean Time'. An island with a lighthouse on it!

However, I did now observe my drift with great care, checking it time after time by looking back over the tail-plane at the island, and however wrong in observing it I had been at the start, I felt certain I was right now; it was 25°.

Out over the sea the clouds began to thin, and grew cleaner, as though it was only the land that had dirtied them; presently they became snowy white, steadily dwindled, and at last evaporated altogether. The fifth thousand took thirty-one minutes to climb. At 5,000 feet I stopped climbing and levelled the seaplane; but the speed only increased by five miles an hour, as far as I could judge from the rough speed-indicator out on the wing-strut, which had most of its scale and numbers worn off. It read sixty miles an hour, but I added five to that, because I knew it lagged at higher speeds. The dashboard speed-indicator was out of action again, its needle jumping about erratically between 0 and 100.

The seaplane was flying twelve miles an hour slower, keeping at that height, than it would have done at sea-level; and, so far, I had gained nothing; for the drift had not lessened by a single degree. Yet I had a stupid reluctance to descend after the long climb, and fondly hoped I should soon pick up a strong westerly that would more than compensate me. I did not care enough to spur my brain into activity; I felt soothed by flying once again, and lulled by being over the sea, a hundred miles from any land. I drew out the chicken from under the seat and ate it with gusto; was not troubled when I broke half a tooth on it, and when it was finished thought, 'Well, that's one heathen converted into a good Christian, at any rate'.

The sea, which for the first eighty miles had been a dirty yellow, was now a dull, dark blue; I was looking down on it when I was astonished to see five enormous rollers or swells reaching out of sight north and south, like slowly travelling weals across the comparatively smooth ocean. I looked all round but there was nothing in sight – as if a ship could have started them! – and I speculated for a while on earthquakes, and the possibility of finding that Japan had disappeared.

Two hours out I spotted a steamer; from that height it looked like a black water-bug crawling on the ocean. By its smoke I could see the wind was S.S.E. below, and not so strong. The wind up above was S.W. but weak, I thought. I had made no attempt to correct the big drift; to do so would mean flying into the teeth of the wind; but I ought now to decide whether I was going to try to correct it and make for Japan, or change course still further to the north and make for Korea. I would decide presently; I must make my brain work and think it out; I would decide quite soon, but not just yet.

Two and a half hours out from China the seaplane appeared to be no longer drifting off course. Relying on instinct rather than observation of the sea a mile below, I thought I was in a slight westerly. But I felt uncertain of everything. After the chart's showing me I had made an error of 20° in reading drift, I wondered if any of my observations were correct. I supposed I could reach Japan. I hated the idea of Korea, of anywhere but Japan. Well, I would try for Japan, I thought. I could reach it all right.

I changed course 26° to the south.

Three hours out, there did not 'seem to be any wind much' I logged. I was full of doubt; it was unlikely that there should be no wind – after that first drift of 45° and then 25°. I had never before tried judging drift from so high above the sea. I might have been making mistakes. My only chance of finding my position for certain was to take the sun's altitude with the sextant and work out the position from that. But how could I rely on my sextant work? I had not used a sextant for months and had never used one in north latitudes before.

I must do it, though, and before Korea was out of reach. Should I or shouldn't I? The flight felt all right, the work would be a terrible fag. No, I must do it presently.

I was now in clear sky except for a thick hazy belt round the horizon.

The burbling roar from the open exhausts had become a drone in my ears.

At 3 hours 10 minutes out I estimated I had five and three-quarter hours petrol left. Land! Right ahead! The faint purple-blue of distant mountains. I watched it intently – this was unexpected luck, to be across so soon. But after a few miles it became a bank of dark cloud below the horizon. . . . I could have sworn it was land. . . .

I felt drowsy, and my charts were a nuisance; neither of them included all three countries, and they were difficult to handle in the cockpit, it was difficult to plot on the loose wind-blown sheet.

3 hours 50 minutes out; surely that was land ahead? Nothing could be plainer; a high mountain and another just behind it to the right; a line of hills, then low land, then another line of hills, faintly purple. There should not be land there; but there it was.

Ten minutes later I could see through the first mountain; it was all clouds, nothing but clouds.

I flew over a lake of cloud which always broke up at my approach and became a layer of downy white pebbles suspended in the air; I could frequently see the far side of it and the clear sky beyond; but every time I flew there, it had moved far off again.

Suddenly I woke up: the speed-indicator had been reading sixty all the time; what if it were right, and what if there had been a thirty-mile wind against me from the start! I should be only a third of the way across and half my petrol burnt. I had been behaving like a half-witted fool. I must go down to the sea at once and find out exactly where I was, how far I had come, what the wind was at the surface, and whether I could reach Japan flying close to the sea. I could read the wind for sure down low. No more flying in a maze of doubt, uncertain of wind and speed and position! Half my petrol was used up already. An attack of panic urged me to shut off the engine and dive straight down as fast as I could. But I regained control; it would only be adding weakness to folly, to throw away my hard-won height. I had taken four and a half hours to come to my senses, now surely I could wait another half-hour and use the height to keep up a good speed for a short time. I pressed the control-stick forward gently, till the speed rose from sixty to 100. The spare height enabled me to keep that speed up for the half-hour. Under the lake of cloud, I entered a belt of close hot air. At 800 feet altitude I levelled the seaplane; I could make no mistake in reading the ocean-surface at that height. There was not a breath stirring below, and the rough water was only the lashed up sea of some distant wind.

So, unless I flew into another contrary wind I had enough petrol to fly 337 miles. Was Japan within that range? Where was I?

It had been hard to think up above, but in this sultry air it was a dreadful labour. How could I use a sextant when I had forgotten all the work. It was simply a waste of effort when I should not be able to rely on the result. I might just as well fly on and save myself the fag of working out a sight. Trust to luck. It would be all right, I supposed. . . .

Well, when I stopped wasting time, perhaps I might start to concentrate. . . . I slipped a cord over my head to secure the sextant.

What figure was it, that must be subtracted in northern latitudes that was added in the south? How quiet and close it was down here, with not a breath of wind, and the sea chopping silently at the sultry air. . . . No, $\gamma$ must be added in the north, not subtracted – add $\gamma$ to colat to obtain $\gamma$. . . . Oh, curse! I should never be able to do it. What was the use? Right Ascension, Equation of time, Hour Angle. . . .

I secured two good sights of the sun between clouds; it was in an excellent position behind my right shoulder and I screwed round in the cockpit for it.

Immediately I brought the sun down to touch the horizon in the sextant, I became absorbed like a hunter. Memory of the art returned in a flash. I quickly read the sextant, then the watch and altimeter strapped on my wrist. I only took two sights; but they were excellent sights; how easy it was! I twisted the resuls out of the slide-rule and roughly plotted my positiont line on the chart. I had 270 miles yet to fly, so I wa-exactly half-way; and had used exactly half my petrol. I could do it only if it remained still air for the rest of the way across; when I should have three and a half gallons to spare. Should I risk it or bolt for Korea? I could not bear the thought of Korea. I held the course; and half an hour later swung 26° northwards again. I was now on the original course, East 1° 50′ North.

Every minute, the sea quietened down until presently I was flitting in a dead calm over a dull, glassy surface with a faint tinge of burnished copper; and under a dull haze that obscured the sun like a low gauzy ceiling, increasing the oppressiveness of the air. I could not understand the sea so ominously quiet, as though waiting; I doubted its friendliness; felt a stranger to it and lonely. Slowly doubts began to press on me; I had never before tried reading drift from 5,000 feet over a sea; if I had underestimated by 20° at the start, why should not all the subsequent readings be wrong? God only knew where I was. I could not rely on the sextant work. Now I had only three hours petrol left and no land in sight. Was my compass right? Was I running up the strait between Korea and Japan? If I had been an hour's flight further off than the sextant made out, I could not reach Kagoshima. My neck ached with twisting.

Only two and a half hours' fuel left, and nothing in sight anywhere – nothing. Unless I sighted the mainland within an hour, I could not reach Kagoshima. My chart ended a few miles south of Kagoshima; was there a gap in the Ryukyu Islands through which I had passed? I wrote, 'This may be hard, I think. Trust I haven't missed Japan altogether.' I was attacked by crazy suggestions, one succeeding the other, to change course and fly north, or north-east, or south-east; for each change there was an insidious reason why it was my only possible hope, and I was racked by panic urge to turn and fly in each fresh direction of safety.

Land! 10° on the port bow. . . .

An island; what island was it?

Was it one of the Goto Islands, or the Koshiki, or the Ryukyus? But there was no other land near; therefore it could not be in any of those groups.

There was a small island to the south of the bigger. It must be Me Sima, the Asses' Ears. The two Ears would be in line from this bearing, and there was an Asses' nose 18 feet high detached to the south. I was far to the north of my course, my drift readings must have been all wrong. Suddenly I realised the islands were 126 miles from Kagoshima and I was still thirty miles from the islands – altogether more than two hours' flight; and I had less than two hours petrol. I must turn north at once and make for the Goto Islands. It would mean a charge of spying, for certain. Well, I could not help it. What did it matter? What did I care?

At this moment I spotted some small islands twenty or thirty miles to the south of the first group.

But on my chart there were no islands south of the Asses' Ears.

So it could not have been the Asses' Ears, after all. Where in the deuce was I?

It must have been Udsi Sima, two islands and a Chimney Rock detached to the south. By an extraordinary coincidence it was a group of islands exactly the same as the Asses' Ears, two islands of about a thousand feet each and a small detached rock. I was only thirteen and a half miles south of my course. I was as good as across.

I poured myself out a brandy, added water which I now carried in a separate bottle, celebrated the occasion, lit a cigar, and in ten minutes had forgotten all my worries.

Before I reached the coast, the sun was setting behind me; it went down below the horizon in a blaze of coppery red, its rays fanning out in the heavens.

Now I was over Japan, grey rocky hills and vivid, deep green forest.

I began thinking of the geisha girls, that I had heard so much about; I did not suppose I should meet any.

I skimmed a densely forested ridge of little hills smothered in countless Christmas trees. On the other side I found Kagoshima in the dusk at the edge of a purple-tinted flat, beside a smooth expanse of inland water. The beauty of it all made me draw my breath sharply.

I began searching the busy front for a safe place;

there was one area protected by breakwaters, but too cramped; launches and motor-boats were crawling everywhere in it like maggots. And, after Formosa, I was determined not to alight within twenty minutes run of a Japanese launch if I could help it.

All the rest of the water-front was open to the big inland sea; it was quite safe to come down on that, but I must consider the possibility of rough weather getting up during the night. I began ranging the shore for sheltered water.

I spotted a flagged buoy; two men were on it and appeared to be waving the flag. I dived and skimmed close above them; for the twilight was making it difficult to see from any height. The water was teeming with bathers. I flew away.

I found a small reef-enclosed lagoon. Lagoons fascinated me and I banked at once to alight; but as I was about to settle, the floor of the lagoon appeared quite bare of water and scared me off. I kept on telling myself to be extra careful; that it was ten times as hard to alight without an error of judgment after a long sea-flight; but I was enjoying myself, pushed the throttle wide open and listened with exhilaration to the motor roaring afresh, as if it were the start of some thrilling flight. I found a small creek entering the sea at right angles, swooped down, inspected it closely, circled and settled softly, perfectly, on the calm water, coming to rest fifty yards below a small bridge that spanned it. I looked at my watch, 9.55 – I had taken 8 hours 40 minutes. I looked at the petrol-gauge – it showed empty; but I knew exactly how much petrol was left, one and two-thirds gallons.

# CHAPTER XX

## OFFICIALS ARE INQUISITIVE

BY the time three launches packed with Japanese officials, reporters and photographers came swishing into the creek, I had all my gear on a wing-root and the seaplane ready for the night.

I had taxied a few yards to the side of the creek on to a small shallow where two sampans were moored, and for once I was able to wait on a float, and smoke peacefully, without a single shout or curse needed, and feeling a little triumphant – I had moved into water too shallow for the launches and they were compelled to send over a sampan.

I was taken across, and Hayashi Sun, an interpreter began introducing me to all the officials one by one. Immediately after that the questioning began:

'What iss first land of Japan you come, pliz?'

'I'm afraid I do not understand.'

'What iss first Japaniss you see, pliz?'

'Japanese?'

'Yess, Japaniss country, pliz?'

'Oh, my land-fall. Udsi Sima.'

'Where iss, pliz? You will show on map where is, pliz?'

I recited my course mile by mile from Udsi Sima to

Kagoshima. Meanwhile they said I must be taken to the mooring as it had been ordered; so they uprooted the seaplane from its snug backwater and towed it to a large buoy outside. The day ended soon after we left the creek, but Hayashi went on noting down my answers by the glimmer from a lantern.

Hayashi was in himself a very pleasant gentleman; he had a scholarly look and at times an absent manner as if regretting a librarian's chair from which he had been wrenched to deal with me. He was tall for a Japanese – he must have been five feet five inches – and dressed in European clothes with a particularly high starched collar that threatened his ears, a tie like a bootlace, a thin but extensive and straggling moustache, and pince-nez which he constantly adjusted up and down his thin nose. While listening to me he ground his teeth widely like a horse, and when trying to express an idea he seemed in pain as if suffering from congestion of words. The officials plainly thought his English as good as Ben Jonson's, and they all fired questions at him rapidly.

I think every one of them asked me what land I had first sighted, demanded my exact course from it to Kagoshima, and requested me to show him on the chart. At first I thought it was only a matter of every official requiring his own reply to save his face among the others; until they began asking it all a second time, and again and again and again.

Presently, Hayashi introduced a new kind of question.

'What iss your trade, pliz?'

'I am a company director.'

'Ah, so, but you are young man?'

'They are young companies.'

'You have other trade, yess?'

'Well, I am an author, I suppose.'

'So, you write for newspapers, yess?' He brightened up as if there might be something in me, after all.

'No, I write books.'

'Ah, so.' His face clouded over again. 'But you have other trade, yess?'

'No, I've retired from all my other trades, I think.'

'What other trade, pliz?'

'Well, for instance, I was a coalminer once.'

'So, a retired coalminer; then you have pension from Government, no?'

'No.'

'No! But surely you have other trade now, no?'

'Me, no, I don't think so.'

'You have other trade beside these, yes?'

'No.'

He seemed determined that I had, and kept on and on about it until at last, exasperated, I said, 'Well, yes, all right, I have got another trade; I'm a philatelist.

'Filat— you explain what iss, pliz.'

'Well, I carry air-mail; some of it belongs to me and I've been told I shall make money out of it, so perhaps you might say philately is my trade.'

(This required a lot of explanation and was not worth it.)

'But you are aviator, is not?'

'Yes, but not by trade.'

'Why is not?'

'Because I make no money at it.'

A police official and Hayashi fired rapid talk at each other with frequent hisses indrawn through the teeth, and short sharp 'Ha!'s The police officer fanned himself more rapidly as he talked.

'Your trade is that you are officer in army, is not?'

So that was what it was all about!

'No, I'm not an officer in the army.'

'You are a Government fly.'

'I do not understand.'

'You are Government fly from New Zealand?'

'Oh! . . . No, I'm a private fly.'

'You are not officer in army?'

After this had gone on for some time, I thought, 'they say the victim of third degree always confesses in the end, and if they want a confession why not let them have one'. So at last I said – 'Well, I am, and I am not, in the Army.'

The party was electrified.

'Pliz explain, pliz! You *are* officer in army?'

'No.'

'You are not?'

'Well, in a way, yes, I am.'

'Pliz explain, pliz! Pliz explain!'

'I'm in the territorials.'

Long explanation that failed. In the end I said: 'Reserves – I am in the reserves.'

'Then you *are* officer in army yes.'

Yes, no, yes, DAMN them!

Later they started on my aeroplane, engine and gear; but even a worm will turn, they say, and at last I refused to go on answering silly questions about the length of my aeroplane. All my equipment was fully described in my registration, and airworthiness' certificates, my aviator's licence, engine-, aircraft-, and journey-, log-books which they could study all night if they wished – while I had some sleep. It was true most of the licences had expired, but they would never spot that. A dog-licence would have done them as well as a pilot's licence; they knew nothing whatever about aeroplanes or flying, and the fact of their questions being silly only irritated me more.

Then they requested me to open up my baggage on the launch before them all.

'Look!' I said, 'as soon as we get ashore, you can inspect my luggage to your heart's content, and not before.'

They accepted that.

On shore the cross-examination continued while the customs and other formalities were proceeded with. After that there was a lull; I was conducted to a large schoolroom, where a long table was set with plates and sandwiches. I cheered up a little. Too soon. First the table was photographed, then the mayor, the chief of police, and half a dozen other officials one by one, until with the continuous flashlights, it was like a summer storm indoors. Now there was a loud pop, my heart jumped, and we sat down to drink some sweet champagne. . . . Perhaps, after all, one should not blame the Japs for applying the 'third degree'; perhaps it was just their nature, and not to be held against them. . . . Every time we drank, the flashlights went off. We posed in the act of clinking glasses. I praised the wine and another glass was pressed on me. Then I offered a toast to the city of Kagoshima;

and though we had to pose each time, I toasted the Japanese people or their country till the champagne gave out. Perhaps it was just as well that it did, for a glass is as good as a bottle to a flown aviator.

It was now nine o'clock at night; but the day showed no sign of coming to an end. I was handed over to Inoue, who was a police officer, affable, apparently easy-going, smooth-mannered, pleasant and extraordinarily polite. I had never met such politeness. He escorted me to a car and with Hayashi we motored interminably through the narrow ways of a densely settled area. Every now and then I would doze off, only to be jerked awake by another polite question.

We reached an hotel and arrived in state. The entrance to the building was at ground level; once inside, the raised floor was before us like a waist-high stage. A row of smiling damsels knelt there and bowed till their foreheads and palms touched the floor; they then raised their bow until they settled back on their heels. Several times they did this while I had an impression of flowing kimono sleeves on the floor and voluminous billowy coiffures of jet-black unswept hair. Hayashi and Inoue bowed profoundly in response; their heads going down and down until the palms of their hands came to rest somewhat above their knees, and then slid on down as far as the knees. At least three times they did this and at first I was spellbound with the way they remained motionless at the end of each bow as if for a split second of prayer. Then I began to feel foolish; how was I to acknowledge such a welcome? I should cut a ridiculous figure in my dirty old European clothes if I tried to imitate such ballet precision; whereas to go and shake hands after such intricate ceremony seemed dreadful bathos. In the end I bowed to the Englishman's limit – five inches.

My shoes were now removed by incredibly dainty fingers; after which, I felt clumsy and flat-footed in my stockings on the padded floor. They did try to fit me with a pair of slippers from a row of them on the ground; but the largest only just admitted the tip of my toes, the heel biting into my instep.

I heartily agreed with Hayashi's suggestion of a bath; and a delicious little maiden led me, closely followed by the policeman, into an empty room. Here I undressed and *the policeman* wound me into a kimono with a long wide sash; then led me into the bathroom. I looked round while waiting for him to go. There was a square tiled well about three feet deep let into one corner and full of water; bowls and basins and dippers lay about. I waited and waited for the policeman to go; but he showed no signs of leaving. At last the awful truth dawned on me – he was *not going to leave*. He stood there motionless except for his eyes which watched my every movement alertly. I began to feel as self-conscious as a blushing bride, and to increase my embarrassment I had no idea what the Japanese bathing customs were. Was I to dip water from the tiled tank and pour it over me, as they did in the East Indies? Or was it correct to get right in? Finally I pointed to bath, basin and dipper in turn; when I came to the square bath he showed signs of animation so I slipped off my kimono, and sank in to my neck, relieved. But he immediately uttered a sharp cry, another Japanese entered, seized me by the shoulder, and began scrubbing my back with an instrument like a hedgehog on a stick. He must have thought I had not washed for years.

By the time this was done and the man had left I was shaken to the marrow; so far I had only got into the bath – what would happen when I came out? I determined to put the onus of the next move on the policeman; I stayed where I was. The minutes went by; I did not budge. He shifted feet; I sat tight. At last he stepped forward, took a tin dipper and went through the action of emptying it over himself. Good, I filled a tin dipper and emptied it over myself. He immediately seized my poor body, rubbed it furiously with a towel like a door-mat, and wrapped up the remains in the kimono. Outside, I found a row of maidens waiting, and again they bowed to the ground; no doubt as a tribute to my fortitude in the bathroom.

My clothes, I noticed with interest, had totally disappeared.

No longer feeling clumsy-footed in the kimono, I was led to a stunted table six inches high and a cushion before it on which I sat cross-legged. The beautiful, polite, little Japanese maiden, with her charming smile and dazzling white teeth, squatted on another cushion beside me, and from a small porcelain jar kept on filling a tiny bowl that needed delicate holding between finger and thumb.

'*Saké*,' said Hayashi, who returned at this moment. Chopsticks were correctly placed between my fingers by the maiden; she was the sweetest little girl with her firm young flesh and smooth brown skin, her slanting, soft eyes and doll's eyelashes. Then I was turned loose before a trayful of the most formidable dishes I had ever seen.

I lifted the first cover and found a bowl of rice; this gave me a false sense of security which was promptly dissipated on my lifting the second. It disclosed chunks of raw flesh, only just killed by the look of it.'

'Rorf-ish,' said Hayashi.

'Rorf-ish? Ho! rorf-ish.'

'Yess, yess, rorf-ish.'

'Oh! Raw fish!'

'Well,' I thought, 'try everything once!' I secured a piece between my chopsticks.

It had a clammy corpse-like taste that made me hurriedly drain the cup of *saké*; the *saké* did at least have an inorganic flavour – like tepid sherry mixed with methylated spirits.

Unable to face the raw fish again, I tried another lid; the Japanese girl laughing delightedly at my discomfiture, and even Hayashi's look of a harrassed father was occasionally relieved by a luke-warm smile.

A thick, round slice, greyish-white in colour at the bottom of some liquid. I prodded it with a chopstick; it gave to the touch like a dead body and followed the chopstick back. I was completely baffled by this; it was round, like a piece of eel or snake, but could not be either because it was solid and without any bones.

They waited expectantly until I inquired.

'Fish.' Hayashi waved his arms about in the air. 'With many arm.'

'Whew! Octopus?'

'Yess, yess, Octop.'

It slithered from between the chopsticks three or four times; at last I secured it, and by working my jaws from side to side managed to sever a hunk; but when I tried to chew it I failed hopelessly. It was like tough rubber, only without the taste. I hastily replaced the rest of the body and clapped the lid on.

With only two dishes left I began to fear I should go hungry. I drained another cup of *saké* and attacked the next bowl; it was full of something golden-brown and cooked. I tried it; it was excellent; I finished the dish first, before asking what it was.

'Fish,' said Hayashi and drew sinuously with his finger in the air, as a comedian will outline the female form. 'Which twist,' he added.

'Eel!' I cried aghast.

'Yess, yess.'

Still game, but weakening, I lifted the last cover; this dish held small cylinders of rice mixed with odds and ends, and wrapped in a dark material. I was not adroit enough with the chopsticks to break one of these, so I secured it whole, and nibbled at it. It was comparatively harmless.

'Seaweed,' said Hayashi.

Raw fish, octopus, eel and seaweed – should I have been better off in a landplane rather than in a seaplane, after all?

Here the photographers caught up with us again. There was no question whether I wanted to be photographed, and all I could do, tetchy under the camera's eye as they struggled with a clumsy tripod, was to fan myself rapidly. After the photographers had finished, Hayashi and Inoue began cross-examining me again with their unfailing politeness; not only did they repeat all the old questions about my landfall in Japan, where I had crossed the hills, etc.; but they kept on asking me what day I would leave Kagoshima, what hour, what minute; where I was going to, and the hour, the minute I would arrive there. I myself wanted to know where I was to go next, so I called for my chart, and after marking off distances I said 'Kochi'.

'But it is not permit to go to Kochi.'

'Oh, but it is; I have permission.'

I had to ransack my papers to find the British Consul-General's letter; but I was quite right, the Japanese had allowed me an additional alighting-place at Kochi. However, I might have saved myself the trouble; the police had instruction that I was not to touch Japan anywhere between Kagoshima and Kasimagaura (Tokyo), but at Katsura.

'You must go to Katsura, if you cannot reach Kasimagaura.'

It made little difference to me, having no cause to suspect the death-trap Katsura was set with; so I agreed. My difficulty was to stifle my yawns.

At last I was allowed to go to bed; Hayashi, I thought, having stood up remarkably well to the ordeal of five hours nearly continuous questioning. I followed the lovely little Japanese maiden up the stairs; long ago I had decided that Ulysses would have managed to be detained at least a year here. I followed her into the bedroom; a faint rustle made me turn round – the policeman was fanning himself at my elbow. . . .

I began to fear he intended sleeping with me, but no, he left – as soon as the damsel had gone – and I wished him a mother-in-law who would never leave him.

I found that instead of walls, my room was enclosed by thin sliding panels. I slid one, to find behind it another room with a Japanese couple asleep on the floor in the middle; I shut it hurriedly. I only tried one more panel; that was enough.

My own room had a piece of furniture in it, a hideous cumbersome old-fashioned double-bedstead with brass knobs.

I went to sleep instantly, but an hour later awoke dreaming I had been attacked by fabulous dragons, roaring monsters with fiery tongues. I slew one or two mosquitoes which seemed of a particularly ferocious genus, adjusted a mosquito-net which I had not previously noticed, and fell into restless, uneasy slumber.

When I awoke, I groaned; slow fire smouldered under my skin. I dallied with the idea of staying in the hotel for a day; but what would be the good? The Japs would never believe I was tired; doubly suspicious, every official of the district would come in smiling and hissing to question me. How I longed for the uninhabited Aleutians.

But, on looking out of the window, I found it was a glorious still day of late summer; the smoke from one or two tall chimneys too lazy to rise. The sun calmly shed an air of serenity on everything. To be flying round the world on such a day was the perfect adventure.

After breakfast Hayashi and Inoue, pleasant, kind,

affable and polite, had a car waiting, and we drove for miles through streets barely wide enough. Countless Japanese strolled everywhere, and only when the car was at the back of their legs, moved leisurely to the side or into one of the open-fronted shops that crowded the ways. The straw 'boaters' of the men looked odd on top of black kimonos, wooden sandals and fans. The drive was one long, dreadful cacophony from two horns, which the Japanese boy never stopped blowing, pedestrians or no. With an electric horn he sounded dots and dashes, and in spite of knowing it must be Japanese – if a message at all – I could not help continually trying to read what he sent. He punctuated with honks from an old-fashioned rubber-bulb horn, and went on and on and on till the most terrible rages ran through me like white-hot fire, and after three-quarters of an hour it was torture. Yet I could say nothing because the car appeared to have been courteously provided by the authorities.

I was taken to the schoolroom where my camera and pistol were ceremoniously restored to me, and the cartridges solemnly counted into my hand, one by one. Thirteen again! It gave me a jolt. There had been exactly the same number of cartridges at Tamsui but then it had not appeared significant.

The sunlight was balm; the water sparkled, the wavelets lap-lapped the beach and gently rolled the shingle. I felt magnificently lazy, and suggested that the seaplane, lightly dancing at the buoy, should be brought in to the beach so that I could load the petrol from there. This was done and I filled up with tin after tin to the accompaniment of a low murmur in my ears from two or three hundred Japanese watching from the beach. A man and a boy, up to their waists, mostly kept the floats from bumping the shingle; once I, too, slipping off a float, went in up to the waist; at this, a ripple of quiet, polite laughter ran through the crowd. When I tried to give my assistants a tip, they refused with bright smiles; I, not knowing it was the Japanese custom to refuse everything several times, put the *yen* back in my pocket; so the poor fellows had nothing more substantial than a smile from me for reward.

The bay was smooth and the first failure to take off carried me opposite the north end of the town. Here I found myself near a fleet of grey warships. They were anchored, and looked very quiet and sleepy on board. After my first astonishment my feelings were mixed when I saw they were all flying the white ensign; no one that I could see took any notice of the little seaplane among them from the same country.

I took off at the second attempt, with only thirty-two gallons in the tanks.

On leaving the mainland I flew over many islets of steep jagged rock, topped with dark little trees; on the rocks below, the ocean swell burst in a dazzling white smother. I gazed, entranced, at the pure hues that even surpassed the tropics; pale green and vivid green, pale blue and vivid blue. 'Firs and rocks and deep-blue sea,' I wrote in the log.

I now faced a 300 mile sea-flight – solely because I was forbidden to approach the land. But instead of being angry, I was pleased; felt soothed and contented out of sight of land. The ocean was friendly and I skimmed the surface to be close. Somehow it gave me strength. Life was grand, and I, a master, could fly with more than skill, with inspiration; flying had become pure art.

'The flying has got into my blood again,' I wrote in the log. 'Think I must be relieved to have that Shanghai-Kagoshima trip past. Very anxious trip. Strong lazy disinclination to do any navigating these days. First hour's flying not noticeable; slips by so quick. . . . Jap girls very attractive. . . . Can see tins turning round and round; wear grooves. . . . Sleepy again. Rotten night, dreaming all night; never properly asleep, mosquitoes, trains. . . .'

'I certainly do feel much fitter to-day despite bad night. Must be getting away from Shanghai and tropical climate. That chanpagne was good last night. can bear much more readily with receptions if fizz goes with it. Didn't like the raw fish, but thought chopsticks and rice easy. . . . Circled Ganges Maru 3.45. Rainstorm, flying low; something rather romantic about tanking across the sea alone like this. Yakumo Maru 4.40, circled, on same course. At four hours out, changed course to N.E.; strongish E.N.E. blowing last twenty minutes. Land–o, 5.35. Celebrate. Air unsmooth,' here the log ended.

Off the southernmost point, Shiono Misaki, of the main island of Japan I flew into a patch of dark windy weather and in it came upon a rusty old tub of a steamer wallowing in the seas; the *Bellerophon*, Liverpool. The log-line ran out a considerable distance from the high stern before it entered the water; and coming round the stern steeply banked, I nearly caught my lower wing in it. I saw it only just in time; I was watching the ship's cook in his white cap; he had stepped out from some place near the stern and waved a frying-pan at me.

Round the point I flew into fine weather again and began looking for Katsura. It was not given on my chart, but Inoue had marked it in, and told me that it was a small fishing town with a natural harbour. This was all I had to find it by, and the whole coast after Shiono Misaki was honeycombed with natural harbours. Coming to where Inoue had marked the place, I found a perfect harbour and town, an ideal place for a seaplane; but I thought it strange that I could see no sign of any launches out waiting for me. After the reception I had had at a big place like Kagoshima, it seemed peculiar that an isolated fishing village should take no notice whatever. I determined to fly on further before alighting.

Inoue had marked the place six miles too far south. There was no mistaking the launch with one man waving a small flag at me, and another an umbrella.

# CHAPTER XXI

## THE CRASH

KATSURA was a beautiful place like a partly submerged crater on the edge of the coast, where the ocean had entered through a gap at the south end and was nearly through at another gap opposite; and only a jagged rim of precipitous rock separated the harbour from the open sea.

A steamer was lying at a pier beside a small town. Not only were half a dozen launches moving on the water, but also fishing-boats (a cross between a yawl and a junk), sampans, and rafts of timber. These with the buoys and rocks just showing through the surface made me shy of alighting there, and I chose an inlet joined to the harbour by the gap. With its mountainous sides, and running inland, it was like a fjord; a slight swell entered and ruled off the surface in curved lines.

The launches came after me through the gap, which was almost blocked by a solitary jagged tooth of a rock 150 feet high; they detached a sampan which they had towed out.

The quickness, with which it was arranged for them to tow me in, was due to the man with the umbrella, who spoke intelligible English; his name was Suzuki.

The police and Customs officials on board were nuggety brown men, more conscious of their individualities, and less suave, than those of the bigger Kagoshima.

I bridled my anchor-rope to both floats; then climbed up to the petrol-tank in the top wing, from where I had a good view. I noticed some fishing-nets in the harbour full of live fish. The first mooring they proposed for me was close to the peak-rock of the outer harbour-rim. I objected because any wind striking this hill of rock might eddy round it and overturn the seaplane from behind, before it had time to weathercock into the gust. They then moved me a few yards nearer the township; this was not much better, but they declared that they were satisfied it was the best place and refused to take me further from the hill. I scanned the heavens; well, it certainly looked as if the weather, at present hot and sunny with a light wind, would remain fine.

On shore, first my luggage was all examined again, and my camera, pistol and cartridges taken into custody; then I was conducted to a small upper room where we stood round a table and drank a liquid they named cider, but which seemed to me like sickly lemonade. Suzuki invited me to stay with him; I gratefully accepted, and as the heat and carry-over of last night's fatigue made me very drowsy, I asked him if I might have a nap there and then. He took me to his house which was wedged among a streetful of slender wooden shells – many of them with shop fronts, that looked too frail to have stood alone.

Suzuki had two rooms, one above the other, in front,

a courtyard, and two more rooms behind that, also one above the other.

From the street we stepped directly into the front room and found his wife on her knees before a small shrine let into the wall, about three feet high and two broad, intricate, delicate, fragile. 'It is for Booda,' said Suzuki, 'and here we pray to Gard.' His wife took me to the upper room of the two at the back; these were newly built and I was the first person to occupy them, Suzuki informed me impressively; I inferred it was a great honour. The walls were of sliding paper-covered panels, and the floor, of large padded squares of rice-straw, edged with black tape. His wife put down a mattress, I mumbled thanks, and fell asleep.

As soon as I was awake, Suzuki rushed me off to see his new allotment of land where he proposed building. On the way he talked of nothing but the wonderful garden he had made there; until my imagination was full of lotus pools and peach-blossom, and beautiful, black-haired, almond-eyed geisha girls. To my surprise I found the back of it a small precepice overlooking the backyards of some miserable shanties at the harbour-edge; and the front, a dirty miniature gully with two or three caterpillar-riddled peach trees, three feet high, a few starved-looking rose bushes and a gloomy penful of bedraggled hens; though I must admit these laid a wonderful omelette for breakfast next day.

Suzuki Sun was a solidly-built Japanese with a square-framed head, smoothly rounded off. He wore large horn-rimmed spectacles, and constantly twitched his nose under them, as if they tickled; looked under thirty, and astonished me by saying he was over fifty; thought I looked over fifty and was equally astonished to hear I was under thirty. He was the only man there who could speak English; yet, though he had lived in the United States for twenty years, his English was often barely intelligible to me; however, I am bound to admit that he thought mine was rotten.

On our return, Suzuki's wife was cooking a meal on a little brazier, fanning the charcoal into glowing embers. There were no fireplaces in the house. The women, Suzuki's wife, his eighty-year-old mother, his two children of nine and five, and the maid Māchāsa, ate first and humbly, so as to be ready to serve their lords the men. Then Suzuki and I squatted in state at the low circular table at one end of the middle courtyard. Although Suzuki had lived abroad so long, I think I rather shocked him by making way for a woman – his wife – so that she might enter a room ahead of me.

After dinner he fitted me with a kimono and a pair of wooden sandals – because I attracted too much attention in European clothes – and I clogged down the street after him to look at the town.

'Suzuki,' I said, 'I suppose you never heard of a man called Ulysses?'

'Uliss,' he said; 'there was a man called like that who had fish-shop in New York.'

'I wondered if this is the place he had difficulty in sailing past because of the sirens here, the beautiful geisha girls I have heard so much about.'

'Yess, we have geisha here. But not so good for you

TWENTY MINUTES AFTER THE CRASH

to see here, I think. In Tokyo, yess, very beautiful geisha; more used to foreign peoples, very beautiful; you like very much more in Tokyo, I think.'

I sighed and bought an oilskin fisherman's coat for 1 *yen* fifty *sen*.

I watched the Japanese with great interest when they were talking to me through Suzuki. I was curious to know what they thought of me; they did not regard me as a hated, despised foreigner who flew, I concluded; but dissociated me from nationality and regarded me as somewhat supernatural; I was a mystical 'birdman' able to ride on the wind, and they could never quite credit me with ordinary human appetites, could never imagine, for instance, that I might be tired or hungry.

Suzuki was influenced by this attitude of his countrymen towards me; it gave me a glamour which I should not otherwise have had, since he must have seen hundreds of flying-machines and pilots. The result was that he asked me if I would fly him to Tokyo with me next day. I said no, that I should have to leave all my gear behind to carry him; my rubber boat, clothes, anchor, everything. He said the steamer could bring up these things next day. Then I said that in a crash the person in the front cockpit was almost sure to be killed, though the man behind often escaped; that I would not take the responsibility of such a thing happening when I was the pilot. He was obviously disappointed; I could see the war going on in him. And the ceremonial politeness of a Japanese host, weakened by living among white people, was nearly overcome by the Suzuki tenacity of purpose, so unshakable when once his mind was made up; but politeness won, he said no more.

I was glad to return to the house, the edge of the flat wooden sandals cutting into the arch of my foot. The mattress was dragged into the middle of the room, a large green mosquito-net suspended by cords from each corner, and I turned in.

I was trying to read myself to sleep with *Pepys's Diary*; and when his wife caught him in the act with the maid o' work, I looked up to see through the mosquito-netting a gigantic black spider on the ceiling. It must have spanned a good four inches. The thought of sleeping on the floor with that monster loose in the room gave me the horrors; I sprang up, seized my walking-stick, wrapped a shirt round the end and attacked. The spider dropped on the mosquito netting, sidled down it, and was lost in the folds on the floor. I flushed it out of here, and, like a black crab scuttling over rock, it made for the open doorway. There it paused for an instant and seemed to glare at me. I flung *Pepys* at its head; it made a noise like a spit, then disappeared down the stairs with a beastly rustling, sidling scuttle.

About midnight I was on the point of dropping off when they started to work a wheezing clanking pump next door; water poured with great splashing; and to judge by the cries and the laughter, the hauling of tubs and the splashes, the banging of dippers and buckets, the whole family, men, women and girls were taking their baths together in a tub in the middle of the yard. Knowing the importance of studying foreign customs of domestic life, I went to the window, but Suzuki had allowed – mistakenly I thought – a small tree to grow beside the dividing fence and shut off the neighbouring yard from view.

In the morning, when my thirteen cartridges were again solemnly counted into my hand, I had an impulse to throw one into the sea; that thirteen was getting on my nerves; but still, having stuck to them this far. . . .

Fuelling, inspection of the motor, and checking of valve clearances proceeded without event. My gear was stowed as usual in the front cockpit, which then, with the rubber boat and bag of mail now containing a thousand letters, was packed tight with more or less resilient matter. My anchor was picked up, and the seaplane towed through the gap to the inlet adjoining the harbour. Here they dropped the anchor and I took it in. I disposed my log-books, charts and instruments in the cockpit and settled myself in, my safety-belt unbuckled as usual for fear of a capsize in taking off and of being dragged straight down.

I shouted 'Good-bye'.

'Will you make circles round the town?' shouted Suzuki. 'The peoples would like to see your aer'plen.'

I taxied downwind.

Though there was a light swell coming in from the ocean and very little breeze, I thought I should be able to take off with only thirty-five gallons on board. But I failed at the first attempt. When the launch came up to find out what was wrong, I asked them to tow me across to the other side of the fjord. This they did, stopping every few hundred yards to ask plaintively if it were far enough; but I bullied them into taking me well across.

Bump, bump, bump the seaplane smacked the swell-tops; bump, she was off. I headed through the gap between inlet and harbour, still low over the water, but gathering speed. I kept the seaplane low while crossing the harbour. I would circle the village as Suzuki had asked; but could not do so without more height. I therefore decided to fly on through the north gap in the harbour rim, gain the necessary height then return and do the act. All the way across the harbour the seaplane gathered speed. I preferred to gain speed rather than height until flying fast enough to make manœuvring easy. When between the peak rock of the harbour's outer rim and the hill behind the township, I pulled back the control-stick, the seaplane's nose went up and she began to climb sharply. I was looking at the township below on my left; it was a pretty sight with the cluster of roofs at the base of the hill, the sunshine strong on the green harbour-water beneath me, and the fishing-boats drawn up on the inner beach of the north gap before me....

A dreadful shock.... I was astounded.... I had struck the hill....

My sight was a blank.... A small aperture cleared, a hole for sight; through it, far away, I saw a patch of bright green scrub on a hillside.... But it was in the distance.... So I could not have struck the hill.... What? Engine wrenched out? Wings torn off? Bewilderment, sickening failure of everything.... A whirl.... A rushing swirl.... Centrifugal forces wrenching at me.... My sight gone black.... A small glimpse as through a telescope, a round sight, half of sparkling harbour-water, half of roof-tops. . . . Straight before me. . . . Diving at it vertically. . . already doing ninety. 'Well, this is the end. . . . Vague sense of loss – of life, of friends. . . . 'Suppose I'd better try for the water. . . .' Controls. . . . Sight blacked out. . . . Vaguely aware of lifeless controls . . . . Fear quite gone. . . .